CORRUPTION AT THE GRASSROOTS

About the Editors

Dr. N. Narayanasamy has a rich academic background and has specialized in Agricultural Economics, Cooperation, and Financial Management. He has contributed over 60 papers in leading national and international journals. He has conducted and guided many research projects. He has conducted several training programmes and workshops on Participatory Rural Appraisal methods, and has been a Consultant to many departments of the Government, Donors and NGOs. Currently, he is Professor of Extension Education at the Gandhigram Rural Institute. He is also Programme Coordinator of the PRA activities at this Institute. He has over 20 years of experience in teaching and research. His publications include: *Repayment Ethic, Extension in University Curriculum, Participatory Rural Appraisal, Analyzing Community Problems: Tentacles of PRA Methodology.*

Dr. M.P. Boraian obtained his Doctoral degree in Rural Development from Gandhigram Rural Institute and pre-doctoral degree in Rural Development from National Institute of Rural Development. He studied the "Status and Problems of Tribal Women" for his Doctoral programme and was awarded with a Fellowship by the International Labour Organization which he executed in the Philippines, Thailand and Singapore. He has published, edited and contributed papers to 34 books, monographs and training manuals. He has prepared 25 research studies, and published 44 articles in national and international journals and newspapers. He has appraised, monitored and evaluated 29 rural projects funded by Government of India and foreign Donor agencies. He has presented papers in 33 seminars and workshops. He was also associated with Research Projects sponsored by UNICEF, ILO, SIDA, SAREC, Planning Commission and ICSSR. He is a member of several regional, national and international professional bodies. Currently, he is Reader in Extension Education at the Gandhigram Rural Institute and guides M.Phil. and Ph.D. scholars.

Dr. M.A. Jeyaraju is Professor and Head of the Department of English and Dean, Faculty of English and Foreign Languages at Gandhigram Rural Institute (Deemed University). Born on 15.05.1947 in Pondicherry, he studied English Literature at Loyola College, Chennai, earned his Master's degree in English from Madurai University and obtained his Ph.D. in English from Madurai Kamaraj University for his pioneering research work on Indian English historical fiction. He is one of the earliest teachers of American Literature in India and is currently engaged in pioneering research in Micro Level Rural Communication. He has served as visiting faculty in Karnataka and Kerala. He has two books and several research articles and book reviews to his credit. He has guided several research scholars for their Ph.D. and M.Phil. programmes.

CORRUPTION AT THE GRASSROOTS
The Shades and Shadows

Editors

N. NARAYANASAMY
M.P. BORAIAN
M.A. JEYARAJU

CONCEPT PUBLISHING COMPANY, NEW DELHI-110059

ISBN 81-7022-829-8

First Published 2000

Published and Printed by
Ashok Kumar Mittal
Concept Publishing Company
A/15-16, Commercial Block, Mohan Garden
New Delhi-110059 (India)

Phones: 5648039, 5649024
Fax: 091–(11)–5648053
E-mail: publishing@conceptpub.com

FOREWORD

Corruption has penetrated into our polity, bureaucracy, business and finally into our cultural fabric. It is a ubiquitous phenomenon, with its tentacles spread across the breadth and length of both the developing and developed world. Corruption has deep struck roots in every soil from macro to micro level. Eradication of corruption is, therefore, a Herculean Task, haunting the minds of planners and policy-makers in every country.

Corruption in high places even brings down the curtain on governments and causes disaster to the economy. Such incidences are widely projected in the media and the masses are well informed of them. Corruption also exists at the micro level, especially in the process of people availing the benefits of welfare and development schemes. This is rampant in the vast expanse of our rural areas and the poor are the worst affected by this menace.

India has the dubious distinction of being one of the 10 most corrupt countries in the world . At the same time, India also houses a substantial number of the world's poor and the illiterate. Fuelled by ignorance, corruption, therefore, flourishes amidst poverty and the corrupt grow rich. Corruption by the bureaucracy at the micro level remains to be the predominant form at the grassroots level. People paying the bribe are not the rich and powerful but the poor and weak.

Corruption at the grassroots, therefore, makes the poor poorer and the bureaucrats wealthier. This is a sad trend in the rural sector and hence should be stalled forthwith. The workshop on "Corruption at the Grassroots Level" sponsored by the World Bank, New Delhi, has deliberated on this theme threadbare and has come out with viable solutions to stamp out this canker from the rural scene.

Gandhigram Rural Institute is proud of organizing such a workshop on a socially relevant issue confronting the rural poor who were the prime concerns of Mahatma Gandhi. We are grateful to the World Bank for the generous support in organizing this forum and also to the eminent personalities and erudite scholars who shared their valuable thoughts and ideas. I would like to place on record my appreciation for the efforts taken by my colleagues under the leadership of Dr.N.Narayanasamy, Professor of Extension Education, to make the workshop a grand success. I congratulate the editors of this book Messrs.N.Narayanasamy, M.P.Boraian and M.A.Jeyaraju, who have laboured on this useful piece of work.

N. MARKANDAN
Vice-Chancellor

Gandhigram Rural Institute
Gandhigram - 624 302
Tamil Nadu, India

PREFACE

Corruption has become the most talked about political problem across the breadth and length of the developing and developed world. Corruption is the most deliberated upon but least disturbed issue. Corruption is also the phenomenon much decried in theory but widely perpetrated in practice even by the most critical opponents of corruption. Yet another paradox is that those who should axe the corrupt and eliminate corruption are at the helm of affairs and are themselves soaked in corruption. Corruption, therefore, has a fertile ground for flourishing rather than a hostile trend to deter it.

The nexus between the corrupt and the politicians who are more corrupt is, therefore, strong and gets cemented day by day. Caught in the vicious cycle of corruption is the donor agencies who pump in funds intended to promote people's welfare through welfare projects and development schemes. The common man in the countryside is a silent spectator to this social crime committed by politicians and bureaucrats. The academia are concerned about the apalling rate of corruption in the political and developmental spheres.

Donor agencies and the beneficiaries have the common objective of channelling and utilising the funds without leakage for fuller use aimed at people's welfare and societal progress. The academia serves as an automation force liaising between the donors and the beneficiaries and also monitoring the development process in its immediate hinterlands. Gandhigram Rural Institute has effectively been discharging its role as a social monitor of the development process ushered in by the Government, donor agencies and the NGOs.

Gandhigram has dealt with an array of social, political and development issues of regional and national interest such as social forestry, drinking water supply and sanitation, rural energy, bio-farming, wasteland development, adult literacy, women empowerment and so on. In its desire to highlight a politically sentitive issue to the nation and the world and sensitise the society towards organised resistance against serious offences committed by those in command of the polity, economy and society. Gandhigram sought the support of World Bank, which is perhaps the first global level body to rattle up this issue and rank the countries in order of corruption. India is ranked as the 7th most corrupt country in the world.

The World Bank readily came forward to sponsor a national level workshop on "Corruption at the Grassroots: The Shades and Shadows" for two days, which was organised at the premises of the State Institute of Rural Development (SIRD), Maraimalainagar, during December 1998. Erudite statesmen, eminent jurists, young political leaders, enlightened academicians, NGOs and Gandhian workers shared their valuable thoughts and ideas, which have been compiled into the present book. Besides papers on specific topics from the Resource Persons, the participants deliberated on specific themes and offered their ideas and suggestions.

Gandhigram Rural Institute (GRI) profusely thanks the World Bank for its generous funding support to host this workshop. Gandhigram is grateful to the elder statesman and *Bharata Ratna* Sri.C.Subramaniam, eminent jurist Sri.V.R.Krishna Iyer, and rising political star Mr.Sitaram Yechuri for their august presence and radiant speeches, besides a host of bureaucrats, researchers and experts from universities. We also thank Mr.Rajasekaran, Director, State Institute of Rural Development and his team for offering a congenial base to host this workshop.

The editors of this book thank the Vice-Chancellor, Dr. N. Markandan and the then Registrar, Dr.B.R.Dwaraki for extending necessary support and encouragement for the conduct of the workshop and permitting us to bring out this book. Dr.M.P. Boraian, and Dr.N.D.Mani, Faculty Members from GRI as Associate Coordinators and a team of Senior Faculty Members as members of the Workshop Organising Committee rendered valuable service for the successful conduct of the workshop. We thank all the staff of Gandhigram Rural Institute who participated in the workshop and presented their valuable ideas. Technical and secretarial support rendered by Dr.S.Manivel, Sri.B.Baskar, Sri.S.Kannan, Sri.K.Kamaraj, Sri. M. Thiyagarajan, Ms.V.Jerina Mary, Ms.M.Annamary Selvi and a number of others contributed to the fructification of our efforts in the present form.

Gandhigram *Editors*
16 August 1999

CONTENTS

LIST OF CONTRIBUTORS

Sri C. SUBRAMANIAM, Former Governor of Maharashtra, "River View", Kotturpuram, Chennai - 600 085.

Justice V.R. KRISHNA IYER, Former Judge, Supreme Court, 'SATGAMAYA', M.G. Road, Ernakulam, Kochi - 682 011.

Dr. N.MARKANDAN, Vice-Chancellor, Gandhigram Rural Institute, Gandhigram - 624 302.

Dr. N.NARAYANASAMY, Professor, Department of ACE&E, Gandhigram Rural Institute, Gandhigram - 624 302.

Dr. S.MUTHUKUMARAN, Former Vice-Chancellor, Barathidasan University, Lady Willington College Campus, Kamarajar Salai, Chennai -600 005

Sri S.S. NARAYANAN, Chairman, Tamil Nadu Sarvodaya Sangh, 'Sarvodaya' 1, Sriram Nagar, Chennai - 600 041.

Prof. VALAMPURI JOHN, Former Member of Parliament (Rajya Sabha), 120/7, Periar Salai, Choolaimedu, Chennai- 600 094.

Sri B.S. RAGHAVAN, IAS (Retd.), International Consultant, 4, Second Main Road, Nehru Nagar, Chennai - 600 020.

Sri SITARAM YECHURI, Member, Politbureau, CPI(M), AKG Bhawan, 27-29, Bhaivir Singh Marg, Gole Market, New Delhi - 110 001.

Sri R.VARADARAJULU, IAS (Retd.), Former Home Secretary, Government of Tamil Nadu and Secretary, Committee on Corruption,

Government of Tamil Nadu, D-92, Anna Nagar (East), Chennai - 600 102.

Dr. S.N.SANGITA, Professor & Head, Development Administration Unit, Institute for Social and Economic Change, Nagarbhavi P.O., Bangalore - 560 072.

Dr. M.P. BORAIAN , Reader, Department of ACE & E, Gandhigram Rural Institute, Gandhigram - 624 302.

Dr. S. MANIVEL, Lecturer, Department of Cooperation, Gandhigram Rural Institute, Gandhigram - 624 302.

Dr. B. MOHANAN, Reader, Department of Politicial Science and Development Administration, Gandhigram Rural Institute, Gandhigram - 624 302.

Dr. V. RAGUPATHY, Senior Lecturer, Department of Politicial Science and Development Administration, Gandhigram Rural Institute, Gandhigram - 624 302.

Sri.V.A. VASUDEVARAJU, IAS.(Retd.), Executive Director, Indian Institute of Community Development, 6, Sixth Cross Street, Brindawan, Pondicherry - 605 013.

Dr. K.SUBHA, Regional Coordinator, Institute of Social Sciences, Flat No.203, 2nd Floor, Niahant Manor Apartments, 8th Main Road, 9th Cross, Malleswaram, Bangalore - 580 003.

Dr. G. PALANITHURAI, Prof. & Head, Department of Politicial Science and Development Administration, Gandhigram Rural Institute, Gandhigram - 624 302.

Dr. B.R. DWARAKI, Professor, Department of Sociology, Gandhigram Rural Institute, Gandhigram - 624 302.

1

REFORMS FROM TOP AND REVOLUTIONS FROM THE BOTTOM*

C.SUBRAMANIAM

We have assembled here to talk about the problem of corruption. Now it has become almost part and parcel of the society. Perhaps most of us are becoming accustomed to corruption. Just as a leper becomes accustomed to his state of life, we are becoming more and more reconciled to the corrupt state of affairs, even though there is a furore now and then. Take a village. You have got a school there. A teacher is appointed so that the village children may be educated. But, in many village schools, teaching is only a second profession for the teachers. Therefore, even though we establish a large number of schools and our budgets show that, crores of rupees are allotted for primary education, what is the net result? After three or four years of studying there, the children do not know to write a correct sentence. In my view, this itself is a case of corruption – where the teacher receives the salary and does not perform his duty properly. Then there is a feeding programme – providing nutritious meal to the children. How far is it being properly operated? In most of the places the entire allotment does not reach the children. It is taken away by those who are incharge of the feeding programme and those who feed the children have to tackle this problem. This is mainly because of mismanagement. The teacher is being paid by the government. Therefore, he is not dependent upon the goodwill of the people and,

---

* Inaugural address delivered by Sri.C.Subramaniam at the National Workshop on "Corruption at the Grassroots" held at SIRD, Maraimalainagar, Chennai, on December 3, 1998.

if certain things are not satisfactory in the programme, the villagers have no means of redressal. Some distant officer is responsible for that.

Therefore, if the school has to function properly, and, if the feeding programme is to achieve the intended objective, we should transfer the responsibility to the beneficiaries; otherwise you cannot get cent per cent results. Therefore, educated parents in the villages should be made responsible for seeing to it that the school runs properly and the teacher comes to the school every day and remains there throughout the working hours. There should be periodic monitoring. At present nobody can question the teacher. If anyone does, "who are you to question me?" is the sort of response that comes. In the same way, if the feeding programme is entrusted to a group of mothers in the village, I have no doubt that they will not only utilise all the resources which are made available, but will also supplement the resources if necessary, because they are feeding their own children. Therefore, local management of the functioning of the institution is the felt need of the hour.

Then we have the Primary Health Centre, where also we find all sorts of abuses. In Coimbatore District, in one place, there was a complaint about the Primary Health Centre that the doctor does not give free medicine at all. Whoever goes there as a patient is asked to buy the medicine from the shop nearby. So, Dr.Avinashilingam Chettiar asked the doctor why he was doing like that when medicines are supplied for the purpose of free distribution. The doctor immediately broke down and said, "Sir, I am doing it against my own conscience. What am I to do? For the purpose of getting admission in the Medical College, my parents had to borrow more than Rs.50,000 for bribes. Now, I suppose it would workout to much more than 20 lakhs of rupees. And that is a debt which I have to discharge. Even to get posted to this Primary Health Centre, I had to pay Rs.1 lakh. I have to pay this and other debts which I have incurred. What can I do?" See how people are forced to adopt corrupt methods. Therefore, it is the system which has to be looked into.

Corruption at the grassroot level, you say. The schools and Primary Health Centres seem to be the centres of inefficiency and

I have described how a doctor grows corrupt, forced from the very beginning to think in terms of getting unearned money in order to recover what he spent for the purpose of getting this post and for undergoing medical education. Therefore, we have to look into this whole aspect. It is a chain. If you pull a chain, the several links come one after another and this is where an approach of change must start–at the basic level, at the grassroot level–if you know the chain and go to the root of it–and the root of it is mainly political corruption. Unless you tackle political corruption, you cannot remove corruption at any level.

We have had 50 years of development after Independence. We have had Eight Five Year Plans. The 9th Plan is underway. I was Finance Minister of Tamil Nadu from 1952 to 1962 – 10 years. After ten years, when I presented the budget the entire budget could not even reach Rs.100 crore. So I said in 1962, when I was leaving Tamil Nadu, I was not able to cross Rs.100 crore. Today, you look at the Tamil Nadu budget – nearly Rs.10,000 crore. And I look at how things happened when we had only Rs.100 crore. And now, with thousands of crore, what is happening? If you look at the whole of the country, the money which we are supposed to have invested in the various developmental activities has been fully drained, but the result has been very very disappointing, mainly because, in our administrative system, whether a particular job is done or not is measured in terms of expenditure shown in that account. If they spend the money, then they have fulfilled the job. This is unfortunately the case where people say, "I have exhausted the budget."

Unfortunately, today roads are laid in such a way that, because of the inferior quality of the work, once it rains, the whole road disappears. The year before last I was in Trichy, where EXNORA functions. They bargained with the corporation and said, "You are laying the roads through the contractors and therefore, the quality is poor. Give the money to us and we will lay better roads for the people." They showed me the difference between the roads laid by the contractors and the roads laid by them. The cost was the same. Therefore, you will find that, unless the beneficiaries are involved in the implementation of the various projects, the results are disappointing.

I think reforms have to start from the top. Revolutions start from the bottom. Unless people at the top level set an example of honesty and integrity, this menace of corruption is bound to affect the entire society. As it is said in the *Bhagavad Gita,* ordinary people follow the leaders of the society. Therefore, if we are to tackle this problem of corruption, of course, we have not only to do something immediately at the grassroot level, *i.e.,* village level, but, if the whole society is to get transformed and be free from corruption, it has to start from the top. Therefore, it is the men incharge of the affairs of the country who have to set the example.

Unfortunately, today, India is shown as one of the most corrupt countries in the world. This is the state of affairs in the land of Mahatma Gandhi. And we find many Honourable Ministers and, unfortunately, administrators and bureaucrats also have got into the court facing various charges – not all of them, but at least quite a big number. This is the state of affairs and, unfortunately, what do we see there? Even though they are charged with serious offences of having swallowed and looted hundreds of crores of rupees, even thousands of crores, they still project themselves as great leaders because of the money they have. And they dominate in the power politics even though they are facing charges of corruption. That shows the state of the society as a whole. We have, therefore, become accustomed to corruption. And people have begun to worship money and whoever has got money. By what way he earned it is forgotten. He might have been a dacoit and got the money, but the society respects him and he is able to dominate the society. Such people form the very pillars of our society.

All these dignitaries who are in court say that they have not yet been convicted. Unfortunately, this is another sorry state of affairs. Corruption cases go on for a long time. I would caution the judicial authorities. Nowadays, even for small matters, people go up to the Supreme Court, 'stay' is granted and then everybody forgets the case.

Have we had any conviction of any politician till now for the serious charges which have been made against him? No. Therefore, people think and they always say that, since the other political party has come to power, it is a vindictive action which they are taking against them. As far as public men are concerned, who get elected to the legislature? who become Ministers? The standard you have to observe is not whether they have not been convicted. The standard should be if he/she is under mere suspicion. That is the standard you have to adopt for public men. They get the votes of the people. They are placed in positions of authority. For them there is no licence to say, "I have not been convicted." Are you above suspicion? should be the standard you have to observe with regard to public men. And, particularly, when a case is filed, the court frames the charges after seeking the various facts available; the suspicion is confirmed; after that the public man could function as a public man only after he is acquitted and the suspicion is removed. Unless we observe such a standard for men incharge of the public affairs of the country, crores of rupees will be siphoned off by ministers and officers.

A friend of mine brought a car from abroad. It had to be cleared. All was cleared, but to give the final certificate, a clerk demanded Rs.100. My friend was taken aback. But the clerk said, "Sir, you demur about 100 rupees. With this only I am able to maintain my family, whereas, there are persons who are making crores of rupees and they get away with it. If I ask for Rs.100 you complain about it." This is how society has got completely corrupted today and we take it for granted that, without this kind of money, you cannot get things done.

There are two types of corruption: one, where a person pays for the purpose of getting some advantage out of the way. Here the person who gets the benefit and pays the bribe and the person who receives the bribe are equally corrupt. But there are cases where even to get what you are entitled to you have to pay a bribe, because, unless that is paid, you are not able to get things done. So you are compelled to pay a bribe. I think we will have to make a distinction between these two varieties. Those who give bribe for the purpose of getting something to which they are not entitled are equally corrupt alongwith those who receive the bribe.

I hope and trust that this workshop you are holding will bear fruit. It is not as if the facts are not known. The disease is diagnosed in all its aspects. What is important is "public awareness." This is very important. On the basis of public awareness, political will should be mobilised to see that this cancer is removed from the society. And therefore, I would appeal to all those who have assembled here to participate in the seminar to examine how to bring about public awareness against corruption. The various implications of corruption must be investigated. The poor people seem to think: "What does it matter if money is taken away? We are not concerned. After all, crores and crores of rupees which are allocated for the benefit of the poor are drained away." As Rajiv Gandhi once said, when we allocate one rupee for the purpose of reaching the poor man, only 10 paise is received by the poor man. Therefore, it is the whole society which suffers from this cancer of corruption. Let us hope that, while we are suffering from this disease, for our children and grand children, we will take measures so that they are able to live in a much better society – honest society – and we will have men at the helm of affairs who are known for their integrity, without any shade of suspicion with regard to their conduct. I am sure you will be discussing the various aspects of the problem and will perhaps try to project some measures to tackle this problem.

I thank you very much for inviting me to this workshop. I wish a successful workshop, giving some guidance to the society for the purpose of tackling this menace. I am glad you will have Krishna Iyer for this workshop, who was at the highest level in the judiciary and who also continues to take interest even after his retirement to see that justice is done to the people, particularly the poorer section.

2

CORRUPTION IN INDIA

Systemic Solutions for the Systemic Problem*

V.R. KRISHNA IYER

My dear friend Sri. C. Subramaniam, the Vice-Chancellor of Gandhigram Rural Institute, and myself are seriously concerned about corruption and so are the other distinguished members of this gathering, including Sitaram Yechuri, who is the spokesman of the Left Movement in this country, and, I would like to know how he is going to react to the theme of wiping out corruption from India, if he and his partymen were made the Prime Minister and Ministers of this country. It must be remembered that this exercise for two days has been organised at the instance of the World Bank or sponsored by the World Bank. The World Bank suggests a national integrity system to fight corruption, not an international integrity system. Such a system, the Bank thinks, should be politically inclusive and citizen-friendly. This requires a committed political leadership, public involvement and participation in the reform process – participation by civil service unions – involvement of professional groups as well as community and religious leaders. Fighting corruption at the grassroot level demands introduction and effective implementation of methods like transparency in government dealings, participatory approach at every stage of the project cycle, empowering people, invigorating local government, strengthening the local, especially the women's groups and creating awareness among them, ensuring accountability and so on. The kind of literature

* Keynote address delivered by Justice V.R. Krishna Iyer at the National Workshop on "Corruption at the Grassroots" held at SIRD, Maraimalainagar, Chennai, on December 3, 1998.

we have from the World Bank by way of contribution to attacking a corrosive disease which is far worse than AIDS – because AIDS is as yet to conquer India. . . . There is one touch of pitch which makes the whole of India unclean, and that one touch is corruption. India, in the words of Gunnar Myrdal, is a 'soft state'. Gunnar Myrdal said there is some advantage in corruption. Where nothing moves by way of files – they simply stay at one table – he said that, if you offer bribe, at least there is a little locomotion – the file moves on. And therefore, there is, in India, an advantage in corruption.

We must realise the background. One of the important persons we must remember is Mahatma Gandhi – it is Gandhigram Rural Institute which is organising this seminar. The other person, close to my friend Sri. C. Subramaniam, is Rajaji. He was the founding patron of the Rajaji Institute in Hyderabad. It was impossible to buy Rajaji, just impossible, literally impossible. Of Gandhi, it has been said–here is a man whose body has little hold over his soul. If you can apply that to any other, it is Rajaji. Once I offered him a ticket while inviting him to inaugurate the MCC *vs*. India cricket match. His grandchild took one away. He called the child back and said, "This is the Chief Minister's ticket and not Rajaji's ticket and therefore leave it here." He himself did not go to the match. Such impeccable illustrations are difficult to produce today as models or paradigms for others to follow.

One of the means of escape from corruption which is possible is to go to the panchayats. When you go to the top, as Mr. Subramaniam pointed out very cogently, if you go to the top you find that there are only charge-sheets for corruption. But then there must be a distinction between criminal and criminal. Although everybody is accepted to be, like Caesar's wife, above suspicion, among the political criminals there is a new nexus of crime and politics. So, when politicians in power are tackled by the CBI or some other organisation for corruption, what happens is that even the Tribunal becomes corrupted. Because you have got this Vigyan Bhavan, a hallowed place and that is now a criminal court. . . . Nobody protests what is the reason why when someone is already in prison the person is to face a trial and that there must be a case of Vigyan Bhavan being used. Tomorrow, it can be Rashtrapathi

Bhavan. I do not know what will happen in this country. It is time that we waxed cynical about some of these matters – and outspokenly cynical. Otherwise we are not going to tackle them. If we are very decent and respectable in using expressions regarding criminals who abound in this country, we are not going to solve the problem at all.

The other omission, if I may say so, and I hope I will be excused for it. . . . While in the old days too there was corruption – even Kautilya's *Arthasastra* refers to corruption – there were kings who were corrupt. There were, in the early days, some ministers who were corrupt. A very clever minister, very able, extremely able minister like Parampally Govinda Menon was charged with having taken Rs.5 crore. He replied, citing the population of Kerala, "After all I have taken 5 paise from each man; is that corruption?" What kind of argument is this? But, that is all mini-corruption – not micro but mini-corruption. But today, it is not macro but super-macro. Terrible corruption is going on in this world. It is all over the world, and India is part of the world. It is a Third World country and, apart from that, India is a 'soft state', and corruption has accumulated so much.

In those old days, I remember one of the Chief Ministers of Kerala was charged with corruption. They always play with Kerala State. They went to Panditji because the CM belonged to the Congress Party and told him, "The Chief Minister is corrupt. You must take action." He asked them, "What is the amount involved?" "Rs.1 lakh." "Oh no, please go home. One lakh is not corruption. Of you come to Punjab it is Rs.10 lakh, 50 lakh, or 100 lakh. Your are coming to me from petty Kerala and say Rs.1 lakh he has taken. Leave it all. It is all a waste of time."

In this country you have a Public Enquiry Commission Act. Supreme Court Judges are appointed. Supreme Court Judges investigated the Kashmir Chief Minister, the Punjab Chief Minister, the Orissa Chief Minister and various other Chief Ministers and then found them all guilty. When Indira Gandhi lost her power and the Shah Commission was appointed by the then Government of Morarji Desai, who himself was a man of utmost integrity, and Charan Singh, who has various qualities which I should not describe here, what happened was, they brought a Bill, a Special Courts Bill and it was referred, under Article 143, to the Supreme Court to find out whether it was valid or not. That is how I happened to know it. I wrote a separate judgment there. What happened in subsequent years was, precisely what Sri Subramaniam has just referred to. Huge corruption, Himalayan corruption takes place in this country, but, when we go to the court, it takes years and years, 5 years, 10 years and the Himalayan corrupt man becomes the master of the Himalayas because it is everest corruption, the highest of the whole country. Because he becomes a Prime Minister, or a Chief Minister or leader of the Opposition and things like that.

So we want a quick-moving legislative process, and that quick-moving legislative process was the "Special Courts Bill." The Bill was referred to the Supreme Court and the Court said, "You should not pick handpicked judges. The Supreme Court Chief Justice will suggest who should be appointed. Otherwise you will stay corrupt by considering this judge because he is favourable to you, the other judge because he is hand-tied to a particular party – this type of considerations will come up." So the Supreme Court suggested these changes. But no action was taken. The Supreme Court gave clearance to the Bill with certain suggestions for modification. Nothing was done. The Bill was not passed. There was no follow-up. In my judgment I pointed out that the very Cabinet which had approved the Bill under the Special Courts Act included a person accused of huge corruption against whom an Enquiry Commission had been held and the Supreme Court Judge, Justice Iyengar Sabesan, had held that he was guilty. But, then, he was allowed to continue. And he is now in your cabinet and he is also saying, "Yes, we must go after big corrupt people." What irony is this? So, today what happens is, there is not one man in India in politics who will not say corrupt people should be punished. But there is not one man in India in politics who is not corrupt. This is the kind of situation that we have. A great paradox, a contradiction, which cannot be solved.

Now let me come to the Panchayats. There is great hope; Dr.Markandan has a great hope as a Vice-Chancellor; I have great hope, that ultimately, the corrective would come from the common people. But what I find is that Panchayat members themselves become corrupt. In Kerala, in the River Alwaye, where Adi Sankara was taking his mother, on her death, for washing the body and then taking it to the hallowed river Periyar... What happens is, all the sand is quarried. The result is that the neighbouring wells go dry. The result is, lots of money gets into the pockets of Panchayat members. And the municipality says, We put up a notice reading "Please don't take bath in this water where Adi Sankara purified the place'. Now a notice board by the municipal corporation says, "Don't take bath in this water because it is dangerous." Because you say the procedure or phenomenon applies to Ganga.

Rajiv Gandhi tried his best to cleanse the River Ganga to the condition of the old days when dead bodies were floating there, because, when people died, the bodies were set adrift there. Now, if people want to die, they go there, because, take two baths and you are sure of dying. It is so polluted. Now what happens in the Panchayats? Panchayat members themselves have become corrupt, because the sand-wallah quarries sand from the various rivers. We have 44 rivers in Kerala – all minor rivers – not the big rivers like the Krishna, the Ganga and like that. We call them rivers. Actually we must call them rivulets or something like that. Sand is taken away, which is necessary for construction of 20, 50 storey structures, buildings. In Kerala people have small houses or they live in big apartments. But today, if you come to Kochin, it can be beaten only by Bombay, not even by Madras. In every place there are only 10 storey, 12 storey apartments and offices and buildings like that. How do they build them? They need sand. How do they get sand? By digging up from river beds. And what happens to the common people? No drinking water because all the wells become dry and then what happens furthermore is, when the monsoon comes next time, there is flood.

There is no way of protecting the people. This is the situation. This endangers the bridges and the foot of the bridges, the pillars of the bridges. People are taking away the sand and the bridges become insecure. All these dangers are not their concern at all. Similarly, the building built itself is insecure. A 10 storey building collapses and a large number of people die and all that you have is one line in the newspaper – 100 people died on account of the collapsing of a building. You must find out who was the contractor, who brought the sand, arraign them as accused people. Nobody is interested. Because these are rich people. The men who built these 10 storey, 15 storey and 20 storey buildings are also powerful. In fact the municipal corporations impose sanctions. Then the builders go to the government. The government waives the sanctions and the waiver is exploited in many places, including Kerala. That is, waiver of all objections that were raised by the municipal corporations by the government because the government has power of waiver. The result is ubiquitous.

Look at this +2 in the educationally advanced State of Kerala. Kerala is a very advanced State. Subramaniam knows it. He was the Education Minister here before Kerala was separated. He laid the foundation stone for the Brighton College's new building in Thalaichery. Kamaraj was the Chief Minister at that time. I am only trying to say that the buildings which are now constructed, they are all built of corruption. One day I told the Commissioner of Income Tax, who is a man of sheer integrity, "Look at that building." He said, "A beautiful building. One of the best buildings. He is a gold jeweller, gold merchant who has a huge income, and he has built it." I said, "Every brick of that building says, 'You are corrupt.' He was taken aback. He said, "What did I do?" I said, "You should have investigated how this man got money and what are the sources of money, legitimate sources of money." "Sir, what can we do? They produce receipts from various places and those receipts we accept. We can not have social audit of any receipt for such buildings." The result is corruption is connived at by law.

I wrote an article in *The Hindu* about "Legalized Corruption." You know one form of corruption. MLAs were given TV sets. Politics in Kerala cannot afford to give free TV sets to MLAs. It so happened that I criticised this very severely. My leftist friends were there. They considered the matter at the State level and said, "Return your TV sets." This is the tendency. Now Parliament members. Yesterday or so, I read in *The Hindu* an article about the enormous amount of money which is being paid to the Members of Parliament. And, on top of that, we have an artist, fine artist on corruption. We had an MP who would say, "Yes, I will get that done. You don't have to pay any money, only the air fare." So he would collect the air fare to Delhi from Kochi and back home. Then the next man will say, "Please get this done for me." He will take from him also the air fare. In all about 20 persons would pay him air fare to Delhi and back. That is what is happening with regard to Panchayats, because Panchayats are also politicised. Politics and criminalisation go together. But Panchayats are becoming politicised. Therefore, some kinds of corruption can easily have access to Panchayats. Ultimately, we feel helpless. Because if the Panchayats themselves are politicised and therefore, criminalised. . . .

Criminalisation and politicisation are two sides of the same coin. Nowadays – I am not speaking of the old days, the great days when Rajaji and Gandhiji and other Gandhians were sentinels of the nation with regard to corruption. Who was to become the Chief Minister of Kerala-Madras State? – between Rajaji and Prakasam– Gandhiji was asked and he said, Rajaji. To day when I mention this at a public meeting, can you get any Chief Minister who can answer Gandhiji's test? We will have a country without chief ministers. Worse, everywhere this kind of thing is going on.

So what I am feeling is, all this invasion into morality, it is because our moral values have gone. I was telling about +2 in the colleges because the Vice-Chancellor is here. The +2 has been brought into Kerala by the Education Minister as a policy. Because the UGC itself has said that +2 should be part of the school career and not part of the college education. I had my +2 in my college. My intermediate was in the college. But now they say that +2 must be attached to schools, which means that every manager gets an opportunity to appoint new teachers for this +2. And the price in Kerala per teacher appointed is Rs.7 lakh to 8 lakh. He has to pay and he is willing to pay because his salary is coming from the government. The government pays their salary. And how to stop the corruption?

The other day the Anti-Corruption Tribunal was going to be

created. A possible Chairman of the Anti-Corruption Tribunal had come to meet me and we were discussing the subject. He said, "I shall see to it that this shall be wiped out." But the poor man died. Just day before yesterday he died. Very thorough-going man, who fought governments and insisted on a corruption-free society to the extent that the Anti-Corruption Tribunal had to he created. He did and completely dislodged the criminals in the Rajan case. He unravelled the whole thing. On the Bench he himself and Justice Kali did, and then the Chief Minister had to resign. But nothing happens today. And what is worse, what disturbs me most, is not all these. What disturbs me is a new globalisation of corruption.

All corruption is invisibly globalised. Written in golden ink, liberalisation of corruption, privatisation, obviously, of corruption. What shall we do? Every multinational corporation gains access to this country – how? Only by bribing. Not merely bribing by the crude way. They don't come and give you 10 crores of rupees and things like that. Sometimes they do that. At other times, what they do is, they give you a handsome access to Harvard. They will give some promotion in other posts and positions. I am told now that the patents legislation is to be considered in the Parliament. I was told at a discussion, because I happen to be the Chairman of a commission: "Sir, this gentleman is the Secretary in the Commerce Department or Deputy Secretary in the Commerce Department, who prepares the notes. You know he has already been promised a post in the WIPO (World Intellectual Property Organisation). Already he has been promised. He will retire in 6 months and then he will go and draw the huge salary in dollar terms. So he will certainly support the amending of the patents law."

Legislations are now tainted with corruption. What will you do? Some multinationals are coming in through every mega project in this country today. The hungry and the poor will curse them because a mega project means funds. Money from where? From undiscovered resources! That undiscovered territory where some bold people go and return safe, and that is the international. What happened to Anderson? Now that Subramaniam has candidly referred to the judiciary in spite of my company with him here, what I am trying to say is Anderson was Union Carbide Chairman. The Union Carbide has all kinds of safeguards in the US. But, in India, they do not have that and, in Bhopal, there was a great tragedy. He came here to see what is happening. And when he found that a Magistrate had issued a warrant of arrest, he took the next flight and then ultimately the Judges sitting in this case – curious – the Judges were taking considerable interest in settling the case. Whenever a multinational company is involved in a litigation, whether it is a case involving a UK firm or other cases involving United States firms in Third World countries, what they do is, they settle the case, because nobody will know what has happened. If you settle the case, the operations within will not be disclosed. Here, the Union Carbide managed to settle the case. Then they added a condition in the settlement. The court accepted the settlement. They said so many dollars are coming, let us not ask the litigation to go on. Let us stop it. I do not know. It may require some kind of investigation into the Judges. But that is a different matter.

But, for the present, what I am trying to say is that they passed their order saying no criminal case against Union Carbide or Anderson shall be continued. They will be quashed, and no future cases shall be entertained by any Magistrate in India. I walked into the Judge's house and asked, "What is the jurisprudence by which no cases are to be filed against a multinational company like the Union Carbide which has killed one lakh of people in 5 to 15 minutes? How can you say no case will be filed?" The Judge said, "We don't know. There is no jurisprudence. But then the senior advocate who is appearing for Union Carbide said we will give these dollars only if you pass such an order." This is corruption. Or you call it invisible adroitness. The way in which the judiciary is pressurised into concealment – this is what is happening. And a code of ethics for MNCs. The United States has proposed a code of ethics. But then, no United Nations dare come out with a bill or any resolution for ethics to be observed by MNCs. Because that is the precise way they thrive over the Third World countries.

Corruption is a currency of the multinational corporations. Corporate power is corruption plus currency. The same way nobody in India dare say if there is any pollution in the rivers – pollution in our air, pollution of atmosphere – 50 per cent of the pollution in Delhi, 50 per cent of the pollution in Mumbai, or 50 per cent or more in Ernakulam are all due to cars' discharge, trucks' discharge – all kinds of noxious vapours – and we are unable to control them, because if you do that, General Motors will come upon you heavily and we are having all kinds of glamorous cars and they represent progress. Progress of the creamy layer and, what shall I say, collapse of vast masses of the people in this country. This is the contradiction you find. So, none is there who dare approach, let it be Narasimha Rao, let it be Gujaral, let it be Vajpayee, let it be Vajpayee to the power of *n* . . . . There is one common factor which all of them have and that is that international access for the MNCs shall be the rule of life in India, so that they can take away or plunder, whatever, they could lay hands upon, including our rich bio-diversity. This is what is happening. We want to tackle them.

I want to awaken your conscience to that. The question is not BJP *vs.* Congress, it is not Congress *vs.* some other party like BSP, KSP or whatever. The real point is, are you prepared to stand up and say: "MNCs! you shall not subvert our *swadeshi* – what we can produce here?" Poor Gandhi has been not only forgotten. Gandhi has been assassinated inch by inch. No *swadeshi* now. I inaugurated a Swadeshi Conference at the instance of the present party in power in Delhi, and *The Times of India* wrote, "Krishna Iyer hijacked by BJP." I said, "No, I am going to speak on *swadeshi* and am not concerned with the party." And now I find in Trivandrum, as I said the other day, "I am so disappointed, the first thing which has been jettisoned by the present government is *swadeshi.*" There is no opportunity for corruption if there is *swadeshi.* But they will not accept *swadeshi.* They will have international morning and 7 O' clock glitter. They will have this car, the other car. They will have soap that will be like this. . . . Yesterday. I found in *The Week* magazine itself, the title referring to orgasm in women.

Our morals are collapsing, our integrity is collapsing, because these multinational corporations are penetrating into the vitals of this country. And the Panchayat members will be given free copies.

Pharmaceutical industries will collapse now with the new patents law and then what will happen is – our doctors will be given these– "You have your conference, we will support it; we will sponsor the conference; if doctors wish to have other arrangements, that will also be given." But the price for the poor people will be 100 times more than what you have. So it is very important, as Mr. Subramaniam very rightly pointed out, "begin at the top". Begin there, then the moral of the people will gain. One blunder the court has committed is the *Hawala* case. Justice Verma did a heroic thing when he started the Hawala cases. But what happened to the Hawala cases? Where are these judges slumbering? What is happening to the High Court Chief Justice charged with corruption and disproportionate wealth? For 12 years the Supreme Court has stayed. When the Chief Justice came to inaugurate the Bar Association Centenary, and said cases must be disposed of quickly, I was speaking as a felicitation speaker and I said, "Justice, please realise that, in your court, for 12 years, a criminal case for corruption against a Chief Justice of a High Court has been pending and you have no qualms to disturb your conscience." Luckily he went back chastened. Meanwhile he died in London on account of some misfortune. What I am trying to say is, the judiciary is corrupt.

You know charges were levelled against some judges in the Supreme Court and three judges who enquired found them guilty, but nothing happened. What has happened to the Chief Justice who retired? Seven charges were proved. And the question for the Chief Justice above him was to recover the money. It was very very delicate. "Should I say that this man seems to be corrupt?" The Chief Justice of India ultimately said, "I do not want to damage the institution. So I recommend . . . . He recommended. I have known that. I had seen him. So what I am trying to say is that our judges. . . .Mr. Subramaniam was Law Minister. In his time, he would have been horrified if he was told that Judges of the Supreme Court and the High Courts take 3 years or 4 years or 2 years after the arguments are closed to pronounce judgment. Corruption! I call it corruption. It need not be money. But so many people are waiting for judgment from the Supreme Court – to lay down the law – or the High Court to give guidance. But they don't do it. They take 1 year, 2 years. What are we to do with the judges? If we do something there will be protests about the "independence of judiciary."

Now the present government, in all its wisdom, after the Supreme Court agreed to an independent Vigilance Commission or CVC, they have produced a Bill by which they will control the CVC and the CVC will control the CBI. So the ultimate control will be with them (government) and we will all be told the CVC has been appointed. Hoax! We have to go into the details. I don't want to take up more time because every sentence that I utter will be the creation of an enemy. But I would only like to say that the most important problem this country has to face today is corruption. Universally, from Kanyakumari to Kashmir, we have corruption everywhere. Every project – mega project, macro project – is bedevilled by corruption and there is none to check it. And when somebody goes to court, it takes 10 years. Long ago, it was said in America, "Whenever you go to court please take care to see that you write a will as to who will execute the decree when you get a decree." Now, here, we must also say, "My great grandson is also authorised to execute the decree when I get it." That is the delay in the courts.

Long ago, when Mr. C.Subramaniam was the Law Minister, I was Law Minister. Together we were in the All-India Law Ministers' Conference in Delhi. Jawaharlal Nehru inaugurated the Conference. He said, "In my state, i.e. Uttar Pradesh, there are already 48 judges. They want more judges. I want to give them a copy of Parkinson's Law, so that they may understand that the judges will create work for themselves but will not dispose of cases." He also said that delay is the source of corruption and that is true. If you take 3 years and 4 years to pronounce judgment after arguments are over, are not people entitled to suspect you? So we have to have an overall view of the whole thing. Kerala was the first state to have a mark list scandal. All marks, they said, is computerised. They manipulated the computer and some of them are in jail. Very important people were sentenced because of the mark list scandal. Admission for even important ones in institutions/ schools, for LKG/UKG, the rate is Rs.5,000 in Kerala and, if it is 1st standard, it is Rs.10,000. If a teacher is to be appointed it is Rs.5 lakh to Rs.10 lakh. It is a kind of an unlimited pollution that is everywhere. We, the people of India, have to save India somehow.

Let us go to the grassroots and not the Panchayats. It is certainly good, thanks to Rajiv Gandhi, who said, "Power to the People." I preserve his speech in Parliament. Although Stalin and Lenin also might have said the same thing, Rajiv Gandhi said: "Power to the People," and the Panchayati Raj has subsequently come and it has become an accomplished fact. If only we can produce a helping spirit in the minds of the people, that is the way to resist the manufacture of the minds by MNCs. They are seen everywhere. Your TV is one of their advertisement agents now, and your magazines, journals, your dailies are all their men. They are all polluting the minds. Murdoch is everywhere. He will control the news. He will control the views. At one session in Delhi to editors, proprietors and journalists of newspapers, I said, "You are newspapers to a philanderer, the President of the United States, but not to the hungry millions of India. What are you? Where is your patriotism? Where is the patriotism gone? Now struggle for the people's cause. There you will be out against MNCs. Your will be out against corrupt politicians." Are we not ashamed of corruption?

Corruption is irritation, it is a seamless garment which goes on and on and on. Not merely in terms of money, but in many many ways in which corruption can operate. It is very important that we go to the Panchayats and tell them, "The people depend on you, because you are everywhere in the country. You are not directly involved in the huge money making operation of the politicians, MLAs and MPs. Your are humble people, women, Harijan women, scheduled caste women, scheduled tribe women." Tell them, "You are the President of the Panchayat; please save the people – save yourself." Women power must be harnessed. That is very very important. *Dalit* power must be harnessed, so that we may be able to fight the upper castes, what they call the creamy layer of the society. And then alone we have some hope. But more than the

Panchayat members, we will have to go to the gram Panchayat itself that is subsidiary to the Panchayat.

There is another organisation where people meet and in every library and every reading room must also be discussed these issues as they come out. Most of the news – 98 per cent of the news – that we get is all controlled and conditioned and screened by Reuters, Associated Press and entities like them. Petty trivialities are published. On the other hand, the big sharks escape and the small fish get caught. That is why Ralph Nader, in his introduction to a book called *America Incorporated,* said that "the law locks up those men and women who steal the goose from off the common but leaves free the greater thieves who steal the common from the goose." If the whole of the country is involved in predatory operations victimising the country, we don't have any thing to say. The judges feel very comfortable punishing a man for picpocketing but the judges are away when the entire environment is polluted by companies to make huge profits. So it is that I say, the law locks up men and women who steal the goose from off the common but lets free the worst fellow who steals the common from the goose.

We have to put an end to it and see to it that India belongs to the people of India as the Preamble to the Constitution says. Without that we are nowhere. The danger signal is there. The alarm will be sounded. We are succumbing. We are surrendering. The syndrome of dependence is very dark. I want Bharat Ratna Subramaniam and men like him, of his stature, to be heard. Let us have a fresh breath of air coming. A tornado is needed before this country can be saved. Yechuri, I look at you, and I wish this was the beginning, as Winston Churchill said, this is not the end. This is not even the beginning of the end, it is the end of the beginning. The Vice-Chancellor must take the responsibility to have this as the end of the beginning. I don't think it is the beginning of the beginning. Let us go ahead, if we are able to convince the people with our own brand of cures – which is the great difficulty.

The man who lectures most is the most corrupt man. So there is difficulty in choosing a referee in the circumstances. You polluted all our air. We are somehow having no oxygen. Let us find some kind of method by which we can save this country and the Gandhian way of *swadeshi,* the Nehru way of self-reliance and the Indira Gandhi way of preserving nationalisation. We are now operating the dismantling of the public sector so that those people can come and occupy the economic space of India. Ashok Mehta said, "We will not allow Bharat Mata's womb to be inseminated by foreign economic hypotheses." It is our solemn duty, therefore, to stand up patriotically and save this country.

3

CORRUPTION AT THE GRASSROOTS*

N.Markandan

Corruption is rampant in Indian society. We are very much concerned about this. The problem has reached a point where it is very difficult to overcome this. We may attribute many reasons for this. We may say that corruption is unavoidable. But it is not proper on our part to express such helplessness, if we really want to serve this nation. Each one of us and each one of our organisations and the state and central governments have a responsibility to think, act, and, contribute towards eradication of corruption.

In order to eradicate the menace of corruption we have to make radical changes in our social, economic and political structures. Individuals also have to strictly adhere to the moral and ethical codes of social and private life. Above all, there must be a mass movement from the village to the national level to fight against corruption in public life. Radical structural changes and a mass movement alone can abolish corruption.

Decentralisation of political power should be made meaningful by providing more powers to the elected bodies and training to the elected members. There must be transparency in the Gram Panchayats, Panchayat unions and the district bodies in dealing with public funds. The members must be made fully aware of the financial transactions at these levels. There must be proper criteria or qualifications for contesting elections to become members or presidents of the local bodies. Only those who have good conduct and character and a record of service to other people must be elected to the local bodies.

* Presidential address delivered by Dr. N.Markandan at the National Workshop on "Corruption at the Grassroots" held at SIRD, Maraimalainagar, Chennai, on December 3, 1998.

Abolition of corruption is impossible without decentralisation of state level and district level administration. Computerisation of administration can be introduced even at the grassroot level to ensure greater transparency and also to give the public access to information. Mere theoretical discussions and resolutions and appeals will not serve the purpose.

The present election system is the root cause of corruption. It breeds corruption. So, reform in the electoral system is quite essential. Even the present 73rd and 74th Constitutional Amendment Acts make for a complicated election system which is not rational. There is no organic linkage between the Gram Panchayats and the district level Panchayat. Direct election may be essential for the Gram Panchayat Presidents, Ward Members of the Panchayat, Union Chairman and Zilla Parishad President. Election to the Panchayat Union Council and District Panchayat Councils will make things more complicated and give room to the defects of the present-day election system to elect the members of the Legislative Assembly and the members of the Parliament. All the Gram Panchayat Presidents must be members of the Panchayat Union Council and, in the same way, all the Chairpersons of the Panchayat Unions must be members of the District Panchayat. Electing those who are not Presidents of Gram Panchayats and Chairpersons of Panchayat Unions to the councils of the above mentioned second and third tiers is an unhealthy practice. It looks like the 'divide-and-rule' policy of the colonial times.

It is essential to encourage the people's consumer movement at all levels–from village to national level – as watchdogs against corrupt practices at different levels. We must also change the present life style which induces people to resort to all kinds of dubious means to earn more to satisfy their inordinate desires. Our educated population, those who are in power and those who are of the middle and upper middle class, set an example of luxurious life style to the people in the lower strata. Public representatives should so conduct themselves that they set an example of simple life. Spending lakhs of rupees on unnecessary things is quite common in public life today. For incurring these expenses our officials and others in different organisations are indulging in corrupt practices.

It is also quite essential to give a value based education to the children in primary schools, high schools and higher education institutions. The schools and higher education institutions must reform their curriculum meaningfully and link it to real life situations. Moral instruction must be part of the curriculum at all levels. In each district there must be a center run by devoted and dedicated social workers to spread 'good values' among the people and create a mass movement to fight against corruption at all levels. During the freedom struggle, Mahatma Gandhi started *Ashrams* to lead community life, setting an example to others and at the same time involving in rural reconstruction programmes. These Ashrams also gave orientation to the leaders to work for the masses. Today we do not have such centres. We need a handful of centres here and there to create this mass movement against corruption.

4

CORRUPTION AT THE GRASSROOTS
An Overview

N. NARAYANASAMY

Preamble

Corruption is an intricate issue and a complex phenomenon. It is not unique to one country or one institution or one group. It is global in nature though the degree varies. It can be traced through centuries in the recorded history of all countries. Corruption is basically a deviation from a code of conduct laid down in any walk of life. It is a behaviour which deviates from the normal duties of the public role of a person or persons to gain pecuniary or status gains. This includes such behaviour as bribery, nepotism, misappropriation, giving/receiving gift, cheating, fraud, dishonesty, embezzlement, kickback, commission, and so on.

Corruption is regarded as a social cancer. It is not a private but a public vice that completely undermines the rule of law and makes governance impossible. Corruption distorts welfare goals, marginalises development process and material progress, and brings disaster to the wellbeing of the country. It threatens the value system, corrodes the culture and destroys civilized life. It poses a serious threat to democracy and to the very way of life.

Concept of Corruption

There are many definitions of corruption as writers either go in for a comprehensive explication or focus on a single aspect. It is also situation-specific or location-specific or based on various dimensions. Yet most of the definitions relate to behaviour of public servants (officials and non-officials) who may be the subject or the object of corruption. For instance, Susan Rose-Ackerman defines corruption as an illegal payment to a public agent to obtain a benefit that may or may not be deserved in the absence of pay-offs. For Shleifer and Vishny, corruption is the sale by government officials of government property for personal gain. To Robert Klitgaard, corruption is the misuse of office for unofficial ends.

According to the World Bank, corrupt practice is the offering, giving, receiving, or soliciting of anything of value to influence the action of a public official in the procurement process or in contract execution. But a more comprehensive, more appropriate and straightforward definition of corruption at the grassroots is that it involves behaviour on the part of officials in the public sector, whether politicians or civil servants, in which they improperly and unlawfully enrich themselves or those close to them by the misuse of public power entrusted to them. All these definitions speak of corruption by government officials. Many regard corruption as a sin of the government. But actually, it does exist in the private sector too, and, in fact, the private sector is involved in most government corruption.

Types of Corruption

Corruption may be classified on the basis of degree or extent or on the basis of its pervasiveness. Based on the extent, corruption may be categorized into three kinds: petty/survival, grand, and, moderate. Petty corruption is practised by civil servants who may be grossly underpaid and may depend on bribes from the public to meet their basic needs. The grand type of corruption is practised by high public officials who, in the process of making decisions of significant economic value, routinely demand bribes, kickbacks, commissions, shares or other gifts. The moderate type of corruption is practised by well-paid civil servants who fall under middle-income or upper-middle-income group. They don't have any problem in meeting their basic needs. In fact, they have all comforts to lead a happy life. Yet they practise corruption out of greed.

Corruption can be classified as isolated or systemic, based on its pervasiveness. Isolated corruption denotes rare corruption consisting of a few individual acts. Systemic corruption is widespread and is institutionalized. Isolated corruption is easy to detect and punish, whereas, curbing systemic corruption requires political will and commitment.

Forms of Corruption

Corruption is omnipresent. No field is left unpolluted by corruption, especially in developing countries. The tentacles of corruption are widespread and deep-rooted. It is prevalent in economic, political, administrative, social, religious, technological, cultural, institutional, educational and environmental spheres. It occurs in all fields and in all activities. The facets of corruption are many. The more recognized common facets of corruption are:

* Taking bribe
* Giving bribe
* Misusing facilities
* Giving improper access
* Stealing things
* Letting others steal
* Allowing undue favours
* Diluting quality of work
* Taking undue favours
* Accepting poor quality
* Spying for others
* Creating disloyalty
* Sabotaging
* Hiring saboteurs
* Taking unearned salary
* Paying for work not done
* Claiming without delivering
* Granting without receipt
* Manipulating accounts
* Abetting manipulation

There are certain unrecognized forms of corruption too. They are:

* Ignoring responsibilities and being lazy
* Remaining incompetent and ignorant
* Debasing oneself and debasing others
* Polluting environment
* Destroying resources
* Over-consumption of resources
* Taking more than what is needed and hoarding
* Tempting to create waste
* Cheating by word or appearance

While fighting corruption, all forms of corruption should be recognized in their essence.

Roots of Corruption

The roots of corruption are numerous. They are complex in nature. They are not exclusive or independent. They are rather interdependent. Locating the roots of corruption and studying the intricate relationship among the roots of corruption will help fight corruption more effectively. Some of the oft-quoted causes of corruption may be briefly stated.

Poverty has been cited as the cause of corruption. Some argue that without poverty there would be no corruption. There is a point in this argument, for poverty results in powerlessness which provides ample scope for the powerful to exploit the powerless and thereby breeds and reinforces corrupt practices. This is seen more in programmes meant for marginalised sections of the community. Yet, poverty cannot be the only cause.

Inadequate remuneration for public officials is regarded as a contributing cause, especially at the petty level. The government, especially in poorer countries, has failed to pay a living wage to public servants. In certain states in India, with corrupt persons at the helm of affairs, the government has not paid salary to its public servants for months together. In such cases the officials are forced to take bribes to meet their basic needs. They are victims as well as perpetuators of a systematically corrupt government.

Corruption does occur where corruption has become part and parcel of the system. The system cannot function without it. Corruption is a lubricant for the wheels of the system to move. It is institutionalized and a stage has come where corrupt-free officials have no place in it.

Corruption breeds freely without any checks in a rigid bureaucratic system with discretionary power and multiple sources of monopoly power. Robert Klitgaard has designed a simple but vivid model to explain the dynamics of corruption:

$$C = M + D - A$$

where C stands for corruption,
M for monopoly power,
D for discretion, and
A for accountability.

The model may be explained thus: Corruption largely depends on the monopoly power and the discretionary power that an official exercises. Monopoly power is found more in regulated economies; discretionary power is quite widespread in developing countries, where rules and regulations related to administration are either poorly defined or not defined at all and accountability is very weak due to ill-defined ethical standards and poor administrative and financial systems.

Ineffective watchdog agencies may also engender corruption. For instance, where legislatures do not provide adequate mechanism for checks, when the enforcement mechanisms are weak, where the judicial system lacks independence, when the prosecutorial institutions are powerless, and where the non-governmental organizations depend on government funds, corruption raises its ugly head.

Risk-return trade-off in corruption is also a major cause. Officials perpetuate corruption mainly because the benefits of corruption (return) are greater than the consequences of being caught and punished (risk).

The failure of the existing systems and mechanisms to prevent and curb corruption is yet another major cause of corruption. In other words, the systems that are designed to combat corruption are handicapped by certain problems, which include the limits of power at the top, the absence of commitment at the top, uncoordinated and piecemeal reforms, reforms that rely too much on the law or too much on the enforcement, reforms that overlook those at the top and concentrate more on the petty and so on.

Other prominent causes of corruption are self-seeking behaviour, fast declining moral standards in public life, excessive state intervention in the social and economic life of citizens, mushroom growth of welfare and subsidy programmes, criminalization of politics, non-emergence of dedicated leaders to lead a movement against corruption, lack of transparency in official transactions, very low degree of people's participation in the development process at the grassroots, lack of information on development and welfare activities, etc.

Effects

Different varieties of corruption are not equally harmful. In certain cases, it is argued, bribes increase economic efficiency. That is, bribes lower the cost caused by regulations to firms that bribe. It is not so in all cases, especially in rural areas. But, when it becomes a norm, its effects are crippling. The effects of corruption on the country as a whole, which are equally applicable to the grassroots, may be briefly stated.

* Corruption breeds wrong choices. It induces competition in bribery rather than in quality and price of goods and services.
* It restricts the promotion of a healthy market place.
* Systematic corruption encourages officials to demand larger bribes creating a culture of illegality, which, in turn, breeds market inefficiency.
* It undermines democracy, for the corrupt can greatly weaken the authority and capacity of the fledgling state.

* It increases the cost of goods and services, promotes unproductive investment and leads to a decline in the quality of infrastructure.
* It imposes disproportionately high cost on small business.
* It may lead to rise in the cost of administration.

The worst affected are the poor, the resourceless and the powerless. Corruption is rampant in the development projects and programmes meant for the poor. As a result, development inputs intended to promote the livelihood of the poor and to catalyze the development process do not reach them fully. There is a very high degree of transmission loss. The net result is that sustainable development in rural areas still remains a myth.

Wrap Up

Corruption is all–pervasive and poor and developing countries, with few exceptions, have been trapped in the dragnet of corruption. Everyone unequivocally speaks of curbing and eliminating corruption. Yet corruption remains with us; it refuses to go. The main reason is that systematic, consistent and honest attempts have not been made to fight corruption. Combating corruption should focus on reforms of the system. It requires an economic approach with great political sensitivity.

The World Bank suggests a National Integrity System to fight corruption. Such a system, the Bank feels, should be politically-inclusive and citizen-friendly, which requires a committed political leadership, public involvement and participation in the reform process, participation by civil service unions, and involvement of professional groups as well as community and religious leaders. Fighting corruption at the grassroots demands introduction and effective implementation of measures like information empowerment, transparency in government dealings, participatory approach at every stage of the project cycle, empowering people, invigorating local government, strengthening local groups, especially women's groups, and creating awareness among them, ensuring accountability and so on.

REFERENCES

Kindra, G.S. and Rick Stapenhurst. *Social Marketing Strategies to Fight Corruption.* Washington: EDI Working Papers, World Bank, 1998.

Klitgaard, R. *Cleaning up and Invigorating the Civil Service.* Washington: Operation Evaluation Department, World Bank, November 1976.

— – , "International Cooperation against Corruption." *Span*, Sep. Oct. 1998: 38-41.

Langseth, Petter, Rick Stapenhurst, and Jeremy Pope. *The Role of National Integrity System in Fighting Corruption.* Washington: EDI Working Papers, World Bank, 1977.

Mauro, Paolo. "Corruption and Growth." *Quarterly Journal of Economics.* 109 (1995): 681-712.

Poverty Reduction and Economic Management Network. *Helping Countries Combat Corruption: The Role of the World Bank.* Washington: World Bank, 1997.

Raj, K.N. "Corruption in Public Life." *The Hindu,* Nov.11 and 12, 1997.

Rose-Ackerman, Susan. *Corruption: A Study in Political Economy.* New York: Academic Publishers, 1978.

5

CORRUPTION
Its Dimensions

S. MUTHUKUMARAN

The dictionary meaning of the word corruption is moral deterioration, especially widespread use of corrupt practices, especially bribery or fraud (Concise Oxford Dictionary). Webster's Dictionary gives the following meanings for the word 'corrupt': guilty of dishonest practices as bribery; without integrity; crooked; debased in character, depraved, perverted, wicked, evil; decayed, putrid, infected, tainted. From the foregoing it is to be understood that when bribery or fraud surfaces in a society, moral deterioration, perversion and wickedness follow and, ultimately, the society will decay and die.

The Extent

It is generally believed that corruption in the form of bribery has permeated all spheres of Indian polity. The extent of spread of corruption in all walks of life can be comprehended by the types of jokes found in the magazines. Of course, jokes are exaggerations of what is happening. Some of the jokes are given below:

* "What did they ask in the interview?" (interview for selection of officials).

  "They wanted Rs. one lakh in cash."

* "I complained to the General Manager that the Head Clerk is corrupt."

  "Did the General Manager take action?"

"He asked me, 'How much will you give me for taking action'?"

* "Why do you say that the officer is a good man?"

  "He will never demand more than the prevailing rate of bribe."

* "What is this? In this office on every table a number like 4000 or 5000 or 6000 is written!"

  "That is the monthly target for bribe for the seat."

* "Why is it your Manager is often saying that you should be straightforward; you should act right?"

  "That is his way of reminding us to pay his share of the bribe."

All these jokes indicate to us that, for getting any work done in any office, one has to pay a bribe. This has become so common that it is said that these days, when a father is looking for a bridegroom for his daughter, he not only enquires about the salary but also the average bribe that the prospective bridegroom may get every month.

It is now accepted among politicians that, to succeed in politics, one has to adopt all crooked means. There is a modern verse in Tamil as follows: "When I was running after women, I was called a debauchee; when I plundered, I was called a brigand; when I committed murder, I was called a madman; when I did all these at a time, I was called a leader."

The Tamil Nadu State Government finds it necessary to order central verification of the degree certificates of all those appointed in the last three years as teachers in schools. The names of all these teachers have been in the registers of employment exchanges. The employment exchanges did not get doubts about the genuineness of the certificates? How is it that the officers who verified the certificates and allowed them to join duty did not get doubts? How is it that, in the schools where they are working, they are not found out as unqualified? If the government is moved to verify the genuineness of all the certificates, there has to be a substantial number of teachers with fake certificates; or, in other words, there are a number of unqualified teachers in the state schools. This would, in turn, raise doubts about the level of corruption that may exist in the conduct of the teacher training examinations.

Every weekly magazine publishes at least one joke every week about corruption among policemen. Some of these jokes are given below:

* First thief: You said you have given up stealing; but why have you started stealing again?
  Second thief: It is the police inspector who urged me again and again to reconsider my decision.

* Policeman to wife: Nobody will have good sense like K.D. Kannusamy.
  Wife: What is the news?
  Policeman: As I am retiring from service tomorrow, he has decided to conduct a benefit dacoity tonight.

* "Halo! is it the police station? There is a thief in our house. If you come immediately, you can......"
  "If we come now, can we get our due share?"

* Policeman to Citizen: What are you thinking in your mind? When he is exhibiting the knife and demanding money, how dare you refuse and disturb the peace?

* Policeman to Rowdy: Kapali, I will not hereafter ask even a single pie as my share (mamool) from you.

  Kapali: This is surprising!

  Policeman: Instead of money, I request you to kindly recommend to the police inspector to transfer me to my native place. That is enough.

* Policeman: Give me Rs.500. Go and do something wrong. I won't take action.

* Chinnasamy: From when onwards are there thefts in your place?

  Ponnusamy: From the time the police station was established, there are frequent thefts.

* Police Inspector: Kapali, yesterday evening you were found near the bridge snatching a gold chain from a lady. How dare you do that? You have been given license only to pickpocket in buses.

If one studies the course of development of corrupt practice one will see that the first step is to be lenient with those indulging in corruption. The next stage is when one comes to know that a subordinate is indulging in corrupt practices and asks for and takes a share. The third stage is when the superior officer encourages or drives the subordinates to indulge in corruption and give him a share. The foregoing jokes on policemen indicate to us that there are policemen who thrive by sharing the proceeds of criminals. Or, in other words, among the policemen the corrupt practices have entered the third stage. The fourth stage will be when the average citizen will loose all faith in the State police and have his own protection system.

It has to be realised that it is the court, the police and the teachers who provide the necessary protection against corruption. Those affected go to the police and/or the court and get remedies. The teacher helps in weaning away the young ones from corrupt practices. If these three services get corrupted, the society has reached the point of no return.

Consequences of Corruption

It is often said that corruption is worldwide and therefore, nothing can and need be done. But the consequences of corruption are such that any responsible citizen will think twice before he tolerates any corrupt practice. Every corrupt practice generates unaccounted money; it is the unaccounted money that is used for not only ostentatious spending but also for funding of criminal and underworld activities. After sometime, those with unaccounted money are able to manipulate political decisions. Accidentally, one of them may also become a political leader and capture power with his money power. From the time corruption shows its head to the time political power is captured by a corrupt individual, it is the poor who suffer the most, but not knowing that they are suffering and the reasons for their suffering. Once a corrupt individual captures power, that will be the end of that society unless it wakes up in time to what is happening.

Every society exists on faith; faith of the individual in the other members of the society. A stage comes when there are a number of individuals of the society turning undependable. The government is then required to step in and take action. The government usually imposes controls and nationalises or centralises the activities. This step, though initially it may look to be effective in curbing fraudulent and crooked activities, soon degenerates into an opportunity for growth of corruption. However, in the ultimate analysis, it may be seen that every corrupt practice stems from fear; fear that he may not get through the examination makes the young one to resort to malpractice in examinations; fear that the husband may get angry makes the wife tells lies; fear that the boss may get angry and take action makes the subordinate cover up mistakes. Fear that the present source of income may not continue in the years to come makes one indulge in corruption and amass wealth as the saying goes: Make hay while the sun shines. Thus, it is fear that is to be conquered. These three aspects of corruption namely, faith, Government regulation and fear are briefly discussed in the following.

A Weakness of Indian Society

An inherent weakness of the Indian society, especially the Tamil society, is that it easily believes rumours. It succumbs to the propaganda by evil persons. Last year, a number of private non-banking finance companies failed. Then the newspapers started reporting about the lavish way of life led by the promoters of the failed finance companies. Then the people took it for granted that all such promoters were frauds and pounced on the promoters for immediate repayment. Even a large bank will not be able to pay immediate cash if a substantial percentage of its customers want their money back at a time. Thus, a number of finance companies which were operated on sound principles were closed down by the panic withdrawal of money by the investing public. But no attempt has been made to scientifically investigate the reasons for the collapse of many of these companies. Thus, the scope for young men to enter into a type of entrepreneurial activity has been closed due to rumour mongering and failure to keep an open mind and find the true causes of failures. Thus, a class of financial institutions is now branded without any valid reasons as a fraudulent enterprise.

Government Regulations

Whenever a corrupt practice in any activity comes to light, there is a hue and cry: "What is the Government doing?" The government invariably reacts by introducing a bill providing for regulating that activity with a provision for getting prior government permission for establishing an institution engaged in the particular activity and also for centralising certain aspects of that activity. For instance, when a large number of self financing educational institutions came up, the government insisted on their obtaining prior permission and also centralising the admissions. This has not resulted in the controlling of corruption. If anything, it has increased the scope for corruption; and increased the cost of education in these institutions. The admission procedure is so cumbersome and protracted that people no longer have any energy left to talk about the corrupt practices of the managements, but are happy to join somewhere and settle down for studies. Thus, government control and interference in any activity will never be the remedy to control corruption. As a matter of fact, corruption may often be directly related to the degree of government control and centralisation.

Fear

There was a story in the *Readers' Digest* (January, 1993) about the corrupt practice of a Mayor in the USA. The Mayor called a landscape architect who had been engaged by the city for work in a local park and openly told him to hike the contract and suggested that they share the hiked amount. Even though the architect was in need of the money for the education of his children, he preferred to inform the F.B.I. He had to suffer considerably for this decision. His enemies unleashed a reign of terror by threatening through phone calls; he was threatened that his car would blow up with him; his enemies spread rumors against him. He learnt that those who make public disclosures of corruption often pay a price. But he felt good for what he did.

In this case, for four years the Mayor had extorted about a million dollars from several contractors. But only one contractor, the hero of this story, had the courage to report i.e., he was not afraid.

Resilience of the Society

In a recent article on "Irrelevance of Kerala", T.J.S. George (*Indian Express,* 1.11.98) states, "Kerala's case cannot be corruption and personality rivalries.... The bigger tragedy is that the people seem to have lost their capacity to react, leave alone to rise in revolt...." When people see school girls are enticed away and supplied to VIPs, paddy cultivation dwindles alarmingly, bridges collapse because of reckless sand mining, people in authority themselves hunt down endangered species of animals and do not react and have lost the capacity to raise their voice, then deterioration, decay and death of the society is imminent.

Fortunately, the Tamil society does not appear to have reached that stage. Though old, this society has still the capacity to react. This society has in the past reacted many times, raising its voice against corruption. There was recently a demonstration against the police for not taking action against the rowdies who were terrorising the merchants in the Chennai Triplicane Bazaar area (news dt.30 October, 1998); there was a news item on 24 October, 1998 about the People's Union for Civil Liberties demanding prosecution of police officials involved in the alleged torture and rape of a lady of Alwarthirunagar; when the people of a village found that the teacher of the village school was irregular in attendance, did not teach the students properly in spite of their complaints to the headmaster and higher authorities, they locked the school and prevented its opening. These and similar outbursts and demonstrations are the signs of the society not having lost its sensitivity to corrupt practices and its capacity to raise its voice against injustice. But there are signs of the society falling into the fourth stage of corruption and they seem to have lost faith in the system.

Due to the absence of elected civic bodies over a long period of time, citizens have set up Exnora Clubs for removal of garbage, a sign of loss of faith in the working of municipal services. The leader of the opposition alleges that persons belonging to the party in power have, with the help of officials, indulged in large scale rigging in elections to cooperative societies. Whether these allegations are true or false is not the question. It is a fact that political leaders who are out of power dare to make such allegations against the permanent government officials as a whole, thus shaking the foundations of democratic governance. Such allegations are followed by cartoons as follows:

* News "Businessmen were abducted by criminals posing as customs officials." *Comment by cartoonist:* "Things have turned form bad to worse. These days one cannot distinguish between officials and dacoits."
* News: "Suicide by Chitra: Statement by Police is filed."*Comment by cartoonist:* "Policeman tells the common man: 'Even if we tell the truth nobody believes us'."

It is pertinent to quote here from Thiruvalluvar, a great Tamil poet of the Sangam age: "In a country ruled by a despot, the government asking for money from the public is like a dacoit demanding the possessions from travelling public" (*Kural* 552). There was recently a news item regarding the students of a college in the heart of Chennai indulging in stone throwing and damaging three government buses because they heard a rumour that one of their college mates was taken to the police station and beaten up.

Such incidents, cartoons and statements by leaders bring to the surface a certain degree of distrust that is brewing in the minds of the public about the established public institutions. Before such incidents and observations become the order of the day, the society will have to wake up.

But there is still hope since, in this country, law has not become powerless. When some unsuccessful candidates challenged the appointment of Tax Collectors made in 1989 by the Haryana Government through its State Subordinates Selection Board, the High Court dismissed the petitions. The candidates went to the Supreme Court. Given the nature of the allegations, the Apex Court ordered a CBI enquiry. The enquiry revealed grave irregularities and fabrication of records and the interview for the selection was found to have been a fake. The Supreme Court set aside the selection (News report dt.28 August 1994). Thus, the Apex Court once again asserted the rule of law in this country.

Concluding Remarks

According to *Saiva Siddhanta,* vide *Tirumantiram,* the Tamil Veda, *Patiyinaippol Pasu Paasam Annati*" i.e., like Pati (God), Pasu (Soul) and paasam (the corruption influence) are eternal; i.e., corruption will always exist. It is not possible to eliminate corruption once and for all. It is the capacity of a society to contain corruption that is relevant. A society which does not possess the tenacity to continuously fight against corruption will be wholly corrupted and will one day or the other vanish from the face of the earth. A society which is eternally vigilant, which is capable of cohesiveness and firmness in its principles and which has the capacity to fight for containing the evil of corruption will not only survive for long but will also grow from strength to strength and prosper. But, to develop this capacity, the society requires divine grace. Let us hope and pray for the showering of the divine grace so that we are endowed with this capacity to fight and contain corruption.

6

ROOTS OF CORRUPTION*

S.S. NARAYANAN

Corruption is Pervasive

It is said, "Corruption is the most infallible symptom of constitutional liberty." There is considerable truth in this statement. Since modern states, benevolent or repressive, control the distribution of benefits and the imposition of costs, usually through a bureaucracy vested with discretionary power, corruption follows. In a report on a recent seminar in Delhi, Kautilya was quoted as saying in his *Arthashastra*, "Just as it is impossible to know when a fish swimming in water is drinking it, so it is impossible to find out when government servants incharge of undertakings are misappropriating money."

Controls are irksome, whether elaborate or rudimentary; public and business not only pay bribes to avoid inefficient rules and taxes, they also pay bribes to reduce the impact of all State-imposed burdens, justified or not. Those who have more money than time promote corruption to save time. Ordinary citizens, when forced to choose between corruption and harassment and delays, find corruption more acceptable.

Payments are corrupt when they are made to agents illegally to obtain a benefit or to avoid cost. Corruption is resorted to

lessen costs and delays;
break bureaucratic inertia;
buy scarce commodities or unmerited benefits;
avoid transparency of transactions;

* Most of the specific instances quoted here are drawn from World Bank and IMF Reports.

undermine State Policy;
fight expensive elections, to buy votes and to buy political influence; and,
override legal norms and buy more favourable judicial or administrative pronouncements.

Roots of Corruption

Corruption is not an independent variable, but a symptom of other underlying causes. Widespread corruption is a symptom of inefficient administration.

Some important features of an administration that contribute to corrupt practices are given hereunder.

(a) State allocating scarce benefits: To individuals and firms based on strict legal criteria, rather than on need. In such cases, bribes clear the legal hurdle.

(b) Official apathy: Because of low pay and inadequate monitoring of their performance. In such cases, bribes act as incentive payments. Corruption is associated with the extent of red tape in administration; the amount of red tape is also partly a function of the prevalent corruption.

(c) Regulations, taxes and criminal laws: Governments impose regulations, levy taxes, and enforce criminal laws. Individuals and firms pay for release from or reduction in these costs.

(d) State handing out contracts and concessions: Large contracts, privatisation of public enterprises and granting of concessions to private firms. In such deals, bribes lower the cost of investments and improve long term returns.

e) Judiciary imposes costs: It can impose costs and transfer resources between litigants. Bribes are used to override legal norms.

It was found that, between 1973 and 1983, judicial delays and backlogs in Latin America increased dramatically, creating incentives to pay bribes. Even if judges were not themselves corrupt, clerks in charge of assigning cases and advising judges demanded and accepted bribes. In some Latin American countries, for example, the lack of formal court fees creates incentives for court employees and judges to charge unauthorised fees. Bribes in such situations influence and expedite decisions.

In Eastern Europe and Russia, murders of business people and bankers are common. Many appear to be execution-style killings that are part of a brutal private system of dispute resolution.

(f) Multiple exchange rates and import quotas are frequent sources of pay-offs.

(g) Supply of credit controlled by State: When the supply of credit and the rate of interest are controlled by the State, bribes are paid for access to credit.

(h) Officials' monopoly power to create scarcity either by delaying approvals or by withholding them. Bribes are paid to receive more prompt service or to avoid delays. Bribes are frequently paid by the unmerited to obtain benefit.

In some countries, systematic high-level corruption coexists with strong growth. These are states that have managed to create secure economic environments for businesses by suppressing democratic norms, for a price.

(i) Financing political campaigns: Bribes substitute for legal forms of political influence. Bribery of politicians buys political influence, and bribery by politicians buys votes.

Democratic elections are expensive. Modern political campaigns require enormous sums of money. Campaign funds, legitimate and illegitimate, are needed to survive in politics. Campaign finance laws in many countries are so restrictive that political campaigns are impossible without unaccounted funds. Scandals in France, Italy, Japan, Korea, and the United States on this score in recent years are cases in point. (In the absence of public funding), businesses that have a stake in politicians' decisions are the primary sources of funds. Contributions are kept secret by both firms and politicians, since, invariably, a *quid pro quo* is involved. In France and Italy, political parties are said to be dominated by "business-politicians". Former Prime Minister Kakuei Tanaka of Japan developed a system under which business houses were assigned candidates to fund and elect.

In some countries, the purchase of votes is quite open (Such payments have a long history, going back to the nineteenth century in England and the United States). Although reforms have curbed such pay-offs in most industrialised countries, by and large, they remain a feature of electoral politics. Many countries do not have adequate laws to regulate the private business activities of public servants. In a number of countries, especially in Latin America, discretionary budgetary funds vested in the executive branch of administration are used to buy votes of legislators.

Crime and Corruption

At the July 1989 Economic Summit in Paris, the Group of Seven countries setup the 'Financial Action Task Force' (FATF), whose brief was to prevent banks and financial institutions from laundering the proceeds of criminal activities. "Some governments had told the FATF that they could not implement its 'forty recommendations' for fighting money laundering because to do so would require adopting regulations contrary to the IMF's advice for liberalising financial markets."

"A few years ago, a group of IMF staff went to a small island country to assess economic development. As they walked around the capital, they noticed a surprisingly large number of small banks (more than 100 in a country of less than 1,00,000 people)." A recent study concluded that (among the industrialised countries) a 10 per cent increase in crime is associated with a 10 per cent reduction in currency demand and a 6 per cent reduction in overall money demand–meaning that the monetary transactions associated with crime created its own 'unaccounted' system. After several exchanges, the money gets laundered and surfaces in regular banking channels.

Contempt for the law has a contaminating influence; successfully breaking one law makes one bolder and makes it easier to break other regulations. Concealment of transaction is ensured through threats and corruption at every stage.

Tacit Support

Bribes paid in the course of many international commercial dealings originate in firms headquartered in industrialised countries whose governments call for vigorous anti-corruption campaigns in developing countries. Leading international organizations and Western Governments are not even-handed in their anti-corruption campaigns; they do not attack the bribe-givers with as much vigour as they attack the bribe-takers.

The United States has a law that makes it a criminal offence for a company to pay bribes abroad. However, leaders of many international corporations privately acknowledge that their firms do pay bribes.

Not many years ago, some representatives of Transparency International, a non-governmental anti-bribery organization, requested a meeting with top trade officials in the Government of an European Country. At about the sametime, another team from Transparency International sought a meeting with officials from a leading business association in another European capital. In both cases, the Transparency International teams were rebuffed. Since then, major corruption scandals have been uncovered in these cases. "Germany has no laws on its books to bar its enterprises from paying foreign bribes and permits them to be deducted from German corporate taxes" (Frank Vogl, Vice Chairman, Transparency International, Berlin).

All these payments, of course, cannot be made legally. Large sums of cash pass hands, and need to be kept from public gaze. Cooperation is bought through corruption at every stage. In short, corruption perpetuates itself.

7

POLITICAL AND CULTURAL CAUSES OF CORRUPTION

VALAMPURI JOHN

My paper on "Political and Cultural Causes of Corruption" is not couched in a scholarly vein. It is with reluctance that one has to live through one's experience, though I do not deny there is commonalty at least to some degree in different experiences.

Though corruption is not an exclusive phenomenon found only in India, this hydra-headed monstrosity of corruption is a devious blight on the socio-political life of India. Corruption is as old as the earth. The earliest recorded mention of corruption is found in the code of Hamurabi in the 22nd century BC. The Pharaoh of Egypt, in the 14th century, is reported to have directed that any one accepting a bribe in performing his judicial functions would be put to the sword. *Manusmrithi, Arthasastra, Rajatarangini* and *Harshacharitra* are some of the ancient Indian works which reveal the history of corruption.

Now the definition of corruption has been expanded after scientific analysis of the causes and consequences of corruption. I would confine myself within the limits of political and cultural causes of corruption.

In our political system, there are political bosses and administrators. Atleast political bosses 'govern' the people till they are reelected, but the administrators or bureaucrats virtually 'rule' them till their retirement. Administration as such, from Village Headman *(Thalayari)* to the Collector of a District, and from the District Collector to the Secretary of the State Government, is a vast expanse of officialdom.

If we take the village administration as a case study, for every certificate the villagers take from the Village Administrative Officer, they have to pay a nominal amount. People also have become so insensitive. A new level of immunity has developed. Earlier there was a category of officials who received bribe and did not execute the work. Now, with the new shock-absorbing level, an appreciation has come to stay, wherein the category of officials who take bribe and get things done are applauded. On a close analysis, of why and how does a village level officer get corrupted, one can find the repetition of this unique commonalty in all the departments.

The Incorrigible Power

Throughout civilization, man the creator has become a slave to the creature. First, he devised images for the formless God and man the creator fell a victim to the images of God – after all his creation. Again he invented money, but man the creator was shocked to witness the strange practice of his being negotiated for a price. It was man who laboured out machines; later the creator found to his rude shock that he came to be displaced by the same machines. He only formed the government; he himself became a slave to his own creation.

As such, a person's social stature is measured only by the yardstick of the wealth he possesses. Even in wealth, land has lost its prime position; liquid cash decides the being and becoming of the person. Therefore, at the village level, the Village Headman is enticed by this debased value system to have more money to assert his position in the social ladder.

There are people who venture to say that the poor pay the Village Administrative Officers get is the basic reason for their corrupt activities. My personal experience tells me strongly that such opinion makers are not right. Even if he is paid more, he would continue to be corrupt. One is wealthier or poorer only relatively; therefore, the Village Administrative Officer is not satisfied with higher emoluments because there are other small political bosses and officers who are more well off than he is. Therefore, the relative strength of money in determining the social stature of a person is principally responsible for corruption at the grassroot level.

Moral Standards and Leadership

Religion, elders, teachers, priestly classes and political bosses at the village level do not wield moral influence any more on the village folk. Every villager knows all these affluent classes of the village are qualified only to preach but are not accountable in practice. Therefore, the Village Headman does not walk in the righteous path but falls into the beaten track of corruption.

There is a virtual crisis of leadership in India. A leader, head and shoulders taller than his contemporaries in fighting out corruption, like Mahatma Gandhi or Jaya Prakash Narayan, is yet to be found. Leaders are not on a moral pedestal to fight against the tendentious phenomenon of corruption, since they themselves are corrupt.

Some who are bent upon fighting out erring corrupt officials or politicians are not sincere in their attempts since they fear the public wrath, tinged in ignorance and unqualified political preferences. Despite the colourfull encomiums foreign election experts have heaped upon the Indian voter for his discriminating tendency of punishing the bosses but voting for the party, how can one justify corrupt political bosses and their parties knocking off victory at the hustings?

It is a moot question whether the Indian voter has ever preferred a party for providing a corrupt-free administration or whether he has voted against corruption. Even if a party is crushingly defeated in an election, there is a considerable percentage of voters who have voted for the party defeated. Are they not aware of the corrupt practices of the party routed in elections?

There is not only a silent majority who are not even witnesses to the active campaign against corruption but an 'active' minority who have developed a high degree of tolerance towards corruption, because of their irrational political preferences.

Burden of Extravagance

The Village Headman has to incur strange and sordid expenses to keep his office going. For example, if a Revenue Inspector or a Tahsildar visits his village for his official work, he has to meet all the expenses of the higher-ups. For these unlawful expenses he is compelled to receive bribes and keep the money ready. This is a feudal extension with concurrence. This state of affairs at the village level can be extended further beyond to the level of higher-ups and this same experience can be applied to other departments like police, cooperation, so on and so forth.

Absence of Resistance

There is no resistance from the people. I should admit people are basically corrupt for at least two reasons:

(a) A corrupt person wants to get a favour which he is not entitled to. By bribing an official, the one who bribes or curries favour illegally by and unlawfully is shorn of the moral right to resist corruption.

(b) Though it is true to some extent that petty corruption is prevalent among civil servants of the lower rank due to gross under-payment, enhanced payment may not wean them away from perpetuating their corrupt practices, since, at any provided period, one is only relatively rich or poor.

Individualistic Syndrome

As a speaker in demand, I have always felt my utter in capacity to convince the audience among literates and semi-literates of the debasing influence of corruption in high places. If there is an increase in the price of a cinema ticket, cine-goers do not feel that their pockets have been picked. Since the political boss or a reckless official at the top in a far off place has received a huge amount from the theatre owners, the poor cine-goers are drastically affected.

The loss to the society as such due to corruption in high places is not felt individually, however, convincingly argumentative a speaker is. If a bridge falls apart immediately after its inauguration, no one feels as if he is torn as under. This is all because whatever claims we make, our people are highly individualistic. They are yet to develop a sense of belonging to a society.

Chasm between Ethos and Life

Most of the officials do not want to stand apart and strikingly different. Instead they go the way other corrupt officials prefer to go. If someone is honest, he expects an appreciation from people around and he does not think he has to be honest for the sake of the society he lives in. This sort of 'rewards sybdrome' is the negation of our national ethos, if we have any. The repeated assertion of Lord Krishna on detachment from the results of an action is often used only as a sententious quotation. This is a chasm between our ethos and social life. Apart from administrators at the local, regional and national level, there are the political bosses who make the system corrupt and perpetuate corrupt practices for their survival. It all starts with the elections.

Legal System

There are candidates who bribe the voters. It is a pity it is not easy to prove the corrupt practices under the provisions of the Representation of People's Act. The onus of proof of corrupt practices against an elected candidate is on the shoulders of the election petitioner. The election petitioner is not in a position to collect details and material to prove the corrupt deeds of the elected. 'Of all the people why should I' is the attitude of the people.

In the past 40 years of election, case history is replete with examples to show how the Indian judges are not for pronouncing against the 'will of the people' in the absence of clinching proof against the elected. They would not normally set aside an election. This is not because there is no formidable evidence to prove the elected to have committed corrupt practices, but, in most cases, it is the absence of the judicial will to go against the powerful decision of the people. The method of election, tne process, the way it is conducted, and the forces in play should have convinced our judges more towards holding against the elected on corrupt charges. If the elections are the basis of a parliamentary democracy, then the fight against corruption should start from elections.

Change in Social Order

We have a set of people who are always angry with mosquitoes. We fail to think mosquitoes are the consequences of backwaters. Therefore, we get confused between causes and consequences and the substance and the shadow. Unless there is a radical change in the social order, it may not be possible to root out corruption. In whichever, country there is a difference of an accelerated percentage between the lowest income and the highest one, unavoidable corruption has been the net result.

In India, it has been said that there is a difference of 240 per cent between the maximum wage and the minimum wage. If it were so, one would be weakened in one's fight against corruption, unless something seriously is executed by way of equitable distribution of income. The conspicuous absence of political will to make the social order more egalitarian is one of the basic reasons for corruption. Political bosses themselves, except a few, are for people to remain in abject poverty and abysmal ignorance. They do things which constitute only a face lift and they do not do anything which goes deeper to alter the situation radically. Poverty eating into the vitals makes people powerless and voiceless.

There is no participation of the people in the projects and programmes meant for people. On the other hand, the programmes are imposed on them from above. Therefore, people are neither participants and, as a consequence, nor watch of the programmes. As poverty is one of the reasons that breed corruption, ignorance too has its contribution. There seems to be no awareness among the people that demanding money for the legitimate services that the state should render like appointments to services, conferring benefits on qualified individuals borders on extortion or robbery and looting and nothing short of it.

Corruption does not end the political career of big or small out of public shame. On the other hand, they employ the same money that accrued to them in the illegal manner to fight out corruption cases against them. Either people are corrupt themselves or they are not aware of the devastating effects of corruption.

Misconception of Growth

Corruption, which includes abuse of monopolistic power, cronyism and nepotism, exacts social costs on society. The proposition that corruption should be tolerated as a necessary evil in promoting growth ought to be rejected. The great Chinese reformer Wang An Shih of the eleventh century, in his attempt to stamp out corruption, was impressed by two ever recurrent sources of corruption – bad laws and bad men. Ibn Khadun, during his tenure as a judge, tried to eliminate corruption and considered that the root cause of corruption was the passion for luxurious living within the ruling group. This is also true of the other sections of the society.

Muddle of Issues and Non-Issues

As one explores the political causes of corruption, one is only reminded of the axiomatic finding of Sri Jaya Prakash Narayan. In the last phase of his life, he came to the definite conclusion that politics is not an instrument for social change. When one witnesses the officers and the political leaders steeped in corruption, one is convinced that the corrupt cannot fight corruption since they have no moral right and strength.

Politics, as it stands today, is dazed between issues and non-issues. They start a party; they run it for some time; they meet workers; they contest elections; they become MLAs, MPs and, if possible, ministers. These are all non-issues to the people, when one considers the political process as a means to a fair and just end. If one party MLAs do not sign the papers for the people, after their defeat, another batch would do so. Some set of people are designed to carry on this routine work; but the question is, which is the party and where is the leader who takes on the cancerous growth of corruption as the main plank?

Fighting relentlessly against corruption is an issue and preparing oneself for a political process and living through the same without lifting a finger against corruption is a non-issue. It is a pity most of the parties are more interested in non-issues than in issues. If the political or official machinery which is meant for weeding out corruption is itself deeply corrupt, will it not amount to pipes drinking the water themselves? This is the strange situation we are left in.

Cultural Causes of Corruption

Many people speak of culture. My question is, whose culture do they speak of? In our society, the affluent have a strikingly different culture from the commoners. And India does not have a uniform cultural pattern. In the pluralistic Indian society, it is not possible to have the same, all pervasive and inclusive culture; instead, it is a conglomeration of different cultures and sub-cultures that we have. How does our culture or what we perceive to be our culture contribute towards corruption is an extensive study. For the purpose of this paper, I will think aloud only a little.

Though culture denotes the external manifestations of a refined mind and heart, it is highly difficult to consign these into a water-tight compartment, relegating what we call civilization into oblivion. Inner attributes of culture and external streaks of civilization do defy tailored divisions.

Excessive Exuberance

As such, ceremonies in Indian families are highly expensive. Our people go by a false pride, whether they belong to the poorest or the near-affluent sections. The idea that one has to live within one's means has not entered into the thinking stream of most of the people. Therefore, the artificial deficit in the family budget warrants more 'income' through illegal means.

The moral fabric our culture makes us regard murder, theft, rape and the like as the principal sins but not corruption. In Tamil Literature, which is at least two thousand years old, one can find the classification of five cardinal sins. Our minds have been trained to think that, while they are the principal sins, corruption is not one. This is because corruption has been treated only as a minor sin, since we are not conscious of the debasing effect it has on our society in general and vulnerable sections in particular.

Disregard for the Means

Again our culture celebrates the victorious, without questioning what means they adopted for the victory. As such the consideration of means is totally absent from our system. Leaders like Mahatma Gandhi declared a virtual war against this deficiency. But we are more interested in the academic exercise of Aldus Huxley than in the practical battle of Mahatma Gandhi.

Narrow Perception

We have only a narrow and static definition of corruption. Our culture has made us think of only taking bribe as corruption, not offering it. Accepting poor quality, creating disloyalty, taking unearned salary, paying without work executed, manipulation of accounts and the many offensive spill-overs of corruption are left out from the corpus of corruption.

Since we are discussing recognized forms and unrecognized ones such as polluting environment and over-consumption of resources at social level and ignoring responsibilities and remaining incompetent and ignorant at individual level, our thinking does warrant total extrication from our narrow perception of corruption.

8

POLICIES AND PROGRAMMES DESIGNED TO CONTROL CORRUPTION
Their Effectiveness

B.S. RAGHAVAN

The theme 'grassroot corruption,' to my mind, is a very untenable proposition, because corruption has to be approached, not in a compartmentalised manner in our society, but in a holistic manner. Each aspect of corruption, at each level – government, private sector, civil services, multinational, political – is inter-linked inextricably. Therefore, unless we start with a holistic perception of corruption, we are not going to make headway. We have enough material on corruption. There are Bibles on corruption: The Report of the Santhanam Committee on Corruption, "Corruption in India: Agenda for Action", brought out by the Public Affairs Centre of Bangalore, and the Administrative Reforms Commission's Report of Morarji Desai. There is nothing in them that needs to be mentioned again. Everything that one can conceive of is in those three *Bibles*. There is nothing revolutionary that one can say, but even so I want to make some three or four propositions to this knowledgeable audience which has encountered corruption in all its dimensions in various ways in their daily lives.

The first point is the holistic strategy. Is the parent setting an example? Is the teacher setting an example? Are the doctors, judges, bureaucrats, corporate chiefs setting examples?

The other day, I was in the house of a doctor working in a government hospital. He was there at about 12 noon. The child asked him, "Appa, aren't you to be in the hospital? It is already 12 O'Clock." Then Daddy said, "No, no, it is a government hospital. I need not go on time." At the age of six, the child learns that dereliction of duty is the right thing and, therefore, when she grows up, she will grow up with dereliction of duty built into her genes. So, all of us, if we look within, are failing in respect of our immediate community, immediate family, immediate neighbourhood, in discharging our respective roles and functions. And there is total abdication and total failure.

Kabir Das said, "I went to look for the wicked man and I travelled all over the world, all countries, but suddenly I realised that all that expenditure and energy was utterly wasted and I looked within and I found my quest, my quest was successful." The same thing applies to all of us. This is not to sermonise but to emphasise the moral regeneration of the family. A kind of a total moral regeneration is needed.

The second is the "work culture". I mention a simple point. In the earlier days of administration, in the 50s, inspection was religiously followed. It was sacrosanct. It was absolute. The Collector must visit every revenue office and leave an inspection note; he had to see whether the old inspection notes had been implemented; what were the grievances; what were the things disposed of; what were the pending items; what were the reasons, etc. At each level, and in each department, inspection was religiously observed until the 60s. Every week the Secretaries to Government should call Joint Secretaries, and Deputy Secretaries, and ask them to bring pending files and tell why these files were pending. All religiously done. Of course, such a system may not totally eliminate corruption, nor expedite disposal; but it can lead to "incremental progress." If someone is prone to delay or to be dishonest about hundred files, and if this system is religiously followed, the number of files over which she/he is prone to be dishonest or dilatory can come down drastically. At least 10 people will be benefited without being harassed. Many of such old systems must be revived. Even our Chief Ministers and Chief Secretaries of today are totally unaware of the potential of the regular inspection which was earlier considered sacrosanct.

Third, let us not talk at large. Put one high profile politician – One Chief Minister, one Cabinet Minister – in jail for one year behind bars and let us see the effect that is created in our country. Put one high profile politician, we can put all seminars on the freeze for another 5 years. But we are unwilling to do this. Because we are unwilling to shorten the procedures; why not shorten the procedures? Apart from forming special courts, why not people – forward – looking, aggressive, dynamic people – vote for a law whereby – a simple thing – not more than 2 appeals will be allowed to superior courts? It will be summary procedure and pre-ponderance of probability rather than proving to the hilt will be the deciding criterion. If the judge comes to the conclusion that the preponderance of probability in a case points to the commission of an offence, let him sentence him immediately.

Why are the politicians, who are concerned with the future of the nation, willing to strike and afraid to wound? The young energetic politicians are the saviours and redeemers of tomorrow. They have larger stakes. They should come out, shorten the procedure, make preponderance of probability the guiding criterion, not allow more than one appeal to the next level of court and one more appeal to the next level of court and be done with it all. Adjournment should not be given right up to the Supreme Court. This is not done in a genuine democracy.

Mr. Clinton in the U.S. was accused. He is facing the Congress in 8 months, for it is a genuine democracy. France and Sweden too have genuine democracy. We do not need a dictatorship to do things fast in a democracy. Think of the USA. How fast things move there! Within about 8 months all the investigators reeled up and the accused President is either impeached or not impeached. So put one person in jail and shorten the laws.

The next step is "social ostracism". Why not political leaders who are charge-sheeted be barred from leading or being members of parties? People are charge-sheeted for frauds and scams involving Rs.950 crore or Rs.1000 crore. They are being hailed as *avatars* and can go about being seen on TV. Their personality can dazzle the whole wide world with state protection! I have a feeling that politicians, whether of CPI or the Congress, follow the principle of "you scratch may back; I will scratch your back."

It is ridiculous! You can never, never, never develop a political will by these means. Charge-sheeted political leaders should be barred from leading parties or being members of the parties; they should not be sitting on the right side of the Prime Minister in various meetings. They should not be received by Cabinet Ministers when they arrive in Delhi. People who are charge-sheeted for frauds and crimes involving thousands of crores lead a very happy, go-free life with all 'Z' category security because the charges are yet to be proved. This is not correct. Once a politician or bureaucrat comes under the cloud of suspicion and is charge–sheeted, he must be stripped of all positions. This invariably does not happen because there is tacit understanding of "give and take" among the politicians.

Then, finally, "social mobilization" is the answer. Trade Unions, Civil Society, and NGOs should mobilize themselves without a sense of being abashed, or apologetic about it and the social mobilization must be brought about by people outside of the government. But, unfortunately, they sometimes fail to understand the logic behind curbing corruption. When I want to proceed against a Trade Union member for corruption or dishonesty, the whole Trade Union hierarchy comes to my room and asks me to drop the proceedings. Is the Gandhian method going to be useful in these matters? I have my own doubt Take Indonesia and South Korea – what the students are doing. Take the Philippines – what the students, young people and the women are doing. We have a vibrant youth force in our country. They could play an active role in eliminating corruption.

9

CORRUPTION
Its Consequences for the Economy*

SITARAM YECHURI

I have been bracketed as a politician. Nowadays even we are sometimes ashamed to call ourselves politicians because of the atmosphere prevailing in the country. But, as there are people and people, there are also politicians and politicians well. One can understand that. Today the general sense of disgust with what is happening, particularly with regard to corruption, what is happening in Indian politics? But there are still – I am optimistic that certain systematic changes in the political arena can redeem the situation. All is not lost as far as corruption is concerned.

Before I come to some tangible issues that I would like to raise here, I must at the outset say that I was a little hesitant to come to this workshop which is being sponsored by the World Bank. I have nothing personal against the World Bank. But, fundamentally, the policies the World Bank is pursuing all over the world are absent in many of the Third World countries. When charges were framed against Narasimha Rao, he was the eleventh Head of State in the whole world against whom corruption charges were framed. I mean, it is not a phenomenon that is isolated and confined to India. No. Why this is happening is something that I would like to touch upon, because, I think you must tackle corruption at the macro level and at the top – and that is where political will is required. I don't think much of the corruption at the grassroot level that you find today can be tackled or eliminated. I entirely agree and sympathize with many of the people at the grassroot level who are indulging in

* Speech delivered at the workshop.

corruption. I sympathize with them, not because I condone what they are doing, but because they are cogs in the bigger wheel and sharers of this.

I am sure that an IPS officer can tell us where the various shares go, because I don't know – nowadays that is done right from the local MLA up to the various levels – how police people, when they extort money, will have to pay the shares. It has become an institutionalized system in our country. Now this is at one level a problem, because, when you discuss corruption, there are three distinct levels with which the discussions sometimes get mixed up. There is a moral question involved, that is, a question of honesty and question of morality and whether there is any devaluation of that. What Mr. C.Subramaniam said in the morning about the education system, about various things, yes, at various levels you can find that. But that is only one aspect of the problem.

The second aspect is actually the attitudinal problem of the society as a whole. Why I am raising this issue and where I think there is a scope for social action that is required. . . . There are changes in the perception and attitude of the people against corruption in the last ten years. For example, I can give you one instance. In North India, you have employment exchanges, very close to Delhi, the national capital, where a cyclostyled sheet is put up on the notice board telling people how much they have to pay for what job. Many of us, as political activists, thought that it was outrageous and so it should be protested against. So a demonstration was organized and people's support was elicited. We were all surprised at some people's response. There was a section which said, "Why are you objecting to this?" We asked, "Are not you outraged that you have to pay the money so publicly, blatantly, that is being collected?" But the answer that came from these people was very interesting. They said, "At least now we know how much to pay; and after we pay, if we do not get the job, our money is returned–there is an insurance. This is better than the earlier system where you do not know what has happened to your money." So there is an attitudinal change today which has to be recognized.

It is not merely a question of a moral preaching of better morality and a moral standing or to say that honesty is the best policy, etc.

But there is an attitudinal change in the society that needs to be tackled. And in tackling this attitudinal change – that is where the point occurs very tellingly – it has to be changed from the top and it is not at the bottom that you really have to tackle it. But, I would rather say that it has to be done simultaneously at both ends. How is this to be done?

One area where you find qualitative change in the type of corruption that is practised in India is related to the economic policies that are coming up. During the last one decade, corruption in India has undergone a qualitative change. And this qualitative change comes in directly through your economic activities, a situation which was not there before these new policies came into being. These policies, which Mr. Seshan was fond of calling "LPG" (Liberalisation, Privatisation and Globalisation). Here was a system whereby individual contract to individual multinational corporations could be settled without either transparency or accountability in terms of a uniform international tender that you call for. And once this came into being – Bofors was the first example, over which there was such hue and cry in the country – you can legally have a multinational corporation or a foreign company marking a certain amount of money for services rendered – and that is the official-legal name for corruption – and the siphoning off and the kickbacks that were received. That began with Bofors, under Mr. Narasimha Rao's Prime Ministership. There was then a series of scams.

Each one of them is actually related to this socalled opening up of the economy and all of them, whether it is the Urea scam, or the Sugar scam, it is estimated that something to the tune of rupees fifty thousand crore has been siphoned off through these scams in these five years. Now this is one dimension where you make money. Corruption comes in directly through the deals that you make. The other dimension is the new economic regime that you have created. You liberalise your financial markets to the extent that, today, the US has estimated something to the tune of 250 millions US dollars illegally kept by Indian exporters in banks outside India. In terms of rupees it is a phenomenal amount. This money truly belongs to your capital market, but it is illegally kept outside and the laws are such that there is nothing much that you can do. Cases will be pending for years together and the government is not really interested in recovering the money even with the existing laws.

The third is that much of the share market boom, etc. . . . During the last ten years about Rs.50 thousand crore has been written off by Nationalised Banks as loans that cannot be recovered – non-performance loans – in these ten years. Just look at these dimensions. Once you look at these dimensions, then to put the blame on anybody lower down saying that he has taken a pittance from here and there – that really pales into insignificance. I am only giving you three areas of this new economic policy which have led to this massive amount of defalcation of funds. Now this is where I think we have to put into practice a set of laws which need to be enforced at the macro level. This set of laws in the present new economic dispensation that you have should enforce that no contract in the country can be given except through a tender.

Corruption may be there as well. But such laws will partly minimise it, but only if you have an open tender and, on the basis of that, the contracts are given. These tenders must be made transparent. An effort was made; it is not impossible. During the United Front regime, the laws were drafted. They are still lying on the shelves. It is not that you will eliminate corruption, but, at least, you will reduce the dimension of it. But why it cannot be eliminated immediately? I will come to it subsequently. But you can at least reduce the dimension of the corruption and the huge amounts that are getting siphoned off, if you actually frame such a set of laws at the macro level, where all economic transactions are to be both transparent and accountable. This can be done, including defence purchases, which normally go under the cover of the Official Secrets Act, etc. Even these can be made transparent and accountability can be ensured. So this is one area. I think that must be tackled and concrete measures must be taken.

The other area is the question of political corruption. I remember, about three weeks ago, the Confederation of Indian Industries was having its general meeting. Nowadays even communists are being invited to speak there, because they do not know – given the flux of the Indian political situation, they never know where we would be –

so they also want to know our viewpoint. I was telling them, "If you want to make money, you are in the wrong place. If you come and join my profession your rate of return will be much faster than in any industry today." That is what is happening in the political field where elections are seen today as the source of return on investment, unfortunately. And this is what a few politicians were trying to fight against. I don't want to actually enter electoral politics because politics is much more than mere election. It has got to do with certain social purposes and values. That apart, how do you tackle this problem?

One way of tackling this problem is through electoral reforms in the country. Today the laws are such that there is a ceiling on a candidate's expenditure, but there is no ceiling on or no accountability of the amount the party spends on the candidate. So a candidate can happily be under that limit and claim that the rest of the money he spent is party money. And there is nothing you can do about it in the law. This loophole is to be plugged. All expenditure of any party that is incurred in the election will have to be divided amongst all its candidates and anybody crossing the legal limit will have to be prosecuted. If this change is brought about, I think, a large part of the political corruption that you see during elections – which again I think is the fountainhead for much of the corruption that happens at the lower level – can be checked.

The second area in which we will have to check political corruption is the question of an outright ban on corporate donations to political parties. There is absolutely no reason why India should permit corporations or firms to actually and legally show donations to political parties. It went to the extent in the last elections – that you find the TATAs sending cheques to all recognized political parties saying this is the fund that they are contributing for our election purposes. We received the cheque for a sum of Rs.16 lakh, but we politely returned it to them saying that, if they want to really contribute to the election fund of the country, let them contribute to the Election Commission. Let the government set up a fund which it can then divide among recognized parties, not in cash, but in kind. It can print posters and things like that – various things can be done. But why should corporations be allowed to fund political parties? The moment you do so, the corporations are making an investment for the future – that, when this party comes to power, these are the favours that we require, and if that party comes to power, it does those favours, and through those favours, there is more corruption that takes place. So, if you want to actually plug this loophole, I think these two important reforms, to begin with, will have to be made in the sphere of electoral reforms so that political corruption, as we know it today, can really be checked.

But more important than this are concrete measures in the political sphere. I think it is actually the political will – the will to fight the degeneration of political morality that we are seeing today. It is not really criminalisation of politics that people talk about. I normally put it the other way round. It is the politicization of crimininals that is taking place today. If you look at the major political parties, the choice that the voter has is limited. Assuming that the voter has the freedom to vote at all, that he will do the voting himself, we find that people just do not turn up there at all. Now all these practices, unless we are able to tackle them in an omnibus fashion, I am afraid we will only be doing things that really do not yield much result.

Apart from the economic there is the other area . . . . The lawyer, an individual, who was arguing against Enron was bought– to the tune of Rs.4 crore – lawyer. There are a set of lawyers like that. They were willing to pay that much amount to all of them. So, what we are actually dealing with right now is an amazing dimension. It is no longer in terms of what we pay from our pocket to get a file moving. You are talking in terms of an amount of money that can actually be equivalent to, let us say, the GNPs of small countries like Bangladesh or Nepal or Sri Lanka. That much amount of money the corporations are willing to transfer, to come and control and monopolize our economic assets in the country. So we require laws. There are laws even in countries like Japan and the USA. There are laws on the percentage of expenditure that can be shown under this head called 'services rendered'. In Scandinavian countries, actually, this category is banned. Your accounts are not passed if you show anything under this head. So these are changes that will have to be brought about.

But, when we come down to the grassroots where people's daily existence is at stake, there are many changes that will have to be made. Shri C.Subramaniam spoke on education. I would like only to make a point. He was talking about the devaluation in the consciousness and the conscience of the teachers. Now we will have to bring in certain down-to-earth procedural laws – You ban, let us say, today, the private practice of government doctors. Teachers in government schools and colleges should not be allowed to have private tuition. In much of the schools the children come there, the teacher takes attendance and, he says, "If you want to complete the course, come for tuition at home." This happens in the classroom. At the grassroot level, this is one area where I think both transparency and accountability have not been achieved, but has not really completely been achieved.

We have the Panchayati Raj System in West Bengal, for instance. I will just give you a small example from West Bengal, the only State in the country where more than 50 per cent of the State's development funds are routed through the Panchayati Raj institutions. Since the PWD, the ministries, the contractors, are making money, the only way to stop this practice is to give the responsibility to the Panchayati Raj institutions and our experience has shown that, in these 5 years, they have built the same quantum of roads and bridges and wells with better quality at one-third of the cost. If you go to a Panchayat office, there is a blackboard outside the office showing the amount of budget allotted, work on hand, amount spent, how much is left. This gives the total picture of the Panchayat's programme with total transparency. This can be universalised in the country ensuring transparency and accountability with public check. Once there is transparency, everybody in the Panchayat will know the amount of money received and for what it is going. Secondly, there is an accountability in the sense that the Panchayat Committee, or the President, is now accountable to state that this amount of money is spent, how it is being spent and there is a public check on it. I think this is the greatest insurance against corruption.

If you want to corrupt me we will have to fix at the level that I am used to. First, when the Janata Party Government came to power, actually, the complaint from the industrial houses was: "Your ministers do not know how to take money. Normally we are used to giving lakhs of rupees but these fellows are asking in thousands. So we are a little doubtful whether our work will be done or not." One area which is beating the rate of inflation every year is the quantum of the transactions taking place through corruption.

A legislation is pending before the Parliament. The government has promised to bring it in this session – the Lokpal Bill. Under this Lokpal Bill, elected persons will have to mandatorily declare all their assets and do it annually. This must be imposed upon them . . . . Already there is a big hue and cry. Ninety per cent of the politicians do not like it and, in fact, they will try to sabotage it. As they have done in the past, they will try now also. But this is where public pressure will have to be built up. It is not only the political parties but a big role is there also for NGOs and various social action groups, which will have to be drawn into this process. I think these concrete measures will have to be taken. Though this is an issue on which all of us I think many of us, can dwell and many moral examples can be given.

I urge this workshop should concretize in whatever frame possible at various levels, at the level of macro economic interactions at the level of macro political interactions at the level of electoral reforms and at the grassroot level, some concrete measures through which the situation can at least be arrested, if not arrested at least reduced, so that the economy finally does not suffer. If the economic policy leads to this corruption. . . . We have seen what is happening in Indonesia, what is happening with Suharto and what happened with Marcos in the Philippines. You find how these people have been amassing money through the LPG policies that are being advocated today in the world. . . . One thing is that this sort of policies lead to corruption. They engender corruption. Corruption thrives because of them.

On the other hand, because of corruption, all your economic calculations go awry. There is an inbuilt cost now in every economic project in our country, which is called the corruption cost, and that cost is actually eventually passed on to the consumer. So corruption is not only created by these economic policies but it also has its consequences on the economy, whereby it inflates your costs and puts greater burden on the people. So I think this dimension of corruption can only be addressed if you plug it at the top and these concrete measures, I think, should merit some consideration. I think I will be very happy if this workshop comes out with some concrete, let us say, blue-print or a plan of action by the end of it, so that it can serve as a guideline for many other political and social forces to act by in the future. I must thank the GRI for providing me this opportunity and through them the World Bank for having sponsored this. I think we will have to understand the linkage between why all this is suddenly happening in the last ten years—because of the economic policies that have come in.

10

FIGHTING CORRUPTION

Relative Importance of Legal Control and Administration at the Grassroots

R. VARADARAJULU

Corruption has grown to alarming proportions in public life and services. It exists both in public and private sector. It has spread its tentacles to legislatures, the judiciary, the trade unions, the media and the independent professions like doctors, lawyers, contractors, chartered accountants and teachers. It exists at all levels of the political and bureaucratic hierarchies, undermining the public interest in terms of morality, economic development, equity and welfare.

Our focus will be on corruption at the grassroot level. The government provides for its citizens through its various departments and enterprises services through which the vast majority of the citizens transact with their government. The services provided are either public utility services such as water supply, power, education, public health, community development or regulatory services such as judiciary, maintenance of law and order, taxation, etc.

At the grassroot level, corruption mostly takes the form of speed money to expedite approvals, licences, certificates of the delivery of public services or granting of legal entitlements. Corruption may be voluntary or collusive between the giver and the taker, or extortionate for rendering a rightful entitlement, doing undue favour or desisting from a harmful act. Hands in glove, the lower subordinate officials may share their booties with their higher-ups. Sometimes, for getting lucrative posts, the corrupt subordinates may make a lump-sum payment commuting recurring payments of share in the bribes. The system of *maamool* (regular bribe) has come to stay. The maamool system, like water, finds its own level. So long as the officer demands maamool for a given service, the citizen, regarding it as part of the system, pays it. If he refuses to pay, then he will have to take the royal path of expensive, time consuming, holistic route without being definite of getting the required service in time. It is more unlikely that he will invest his time and resources in fighting the corrupt system because the legal processes involved are also equally cumbersome, expensive and time consuming. The common man has to deal, day in and day out, with these officials and he apprehends rebuke at their hands and gives up fighting the system as not worthwhile.

Corruption at the grassroot level harasses the vast majority of the poor, ignorant rural masses. This tarnishes the image of the government, makes one lose faith in the system and eats away like cancer the polity, economy and society. It is hardly possible for an individual to fight against it. Ironically, the servants, viz., the elected politicians and the bureaucrats, are like masters and the masters, viz., the citizens who elect the politicians, are like servants. The higher bureaucracy seems to be unwilling or unable to tackle corruption at lower levels.

India inherited an administrative system from the British in 1947. It was a power oriented structure tailored to suit the British in ruling the subjugated Indians. The philosophy of governance was founded on suspicion rather than on providing services to the citizen. Article 313 of the Constitution of India provides for the continuance, insofar as consistent with the provisions of the Constitution, of all laws, rules, regulations, orders, etc., made before the commencement of the Constitution. We have inherited not only the same steel frame but also its culture.

This system is based on separate and overlapping functionaries and territorial hierarchies. This institutional structure, by its nature, causes delay in taking decisions, alienates the citizen from the government and is unfriendly. A small farmer, even to get a crop loan, will have to deal with the Village Administrative Officer, Tahsildar, Panchayat Union Commissioner, officers in the Agriculture Department, the Co-operative Department, etc. If he cannot get the loan, he will, on appeal, have to approach the District Agricultural

Officer, the Deputy Registrar of Cooperative Societies, the Project Officer of the District Rural Development Agency and, finally, the District Collector, sometimes, even the Government. An industrialist, to set up a new factory, will have to interact with officers of the Department of Revenue, Local Administration, Town and Country Planning, Labour, Factories, Commercial Taxes, Fire Service, Electricity, Water Supply, Customs, Central Excise, etc. This is only illustrative. Though the departments are separate, many functions are overlapping and interdependent, lacking meaningful purpose, cohesion and vision. The growing size and complexity of government has resulted in an impersonal relationship between the bureaucrats and the common man and this has steadily expanded the scope of corruption. To combat this cancer, fundamental changes in the structure of the government are called for. For effective governance, the changed structure we envisage should be simple, accountable, responsive and transparent. The cost of the change should be commensurate with the tangible and intangible benefits that it is likely to bring in.

To the extent possible, the hierarchical system (i) should be remodelled so that the service provider is closer to the citizen and easier to access for timely delivery of services; (ii) avoid overlapping of functions, defining the standards of service with clarity and fixing accountability of the service provider without any ambiguity; (iii) ensure that, from the point of view of the citizen, for a single service, he does not have to deal separately with various agencies; and, (iv) ensure that, except on policy issues affecting the entire State, solutions to field level problems need not normally go beyond the district level.

The interests of clean administration require transparency and accessibility to all documentation of government work, barring, of course, matters relating to national defence, security and integrity of the country. The underlying philosophy of the Official Secrets Act 1923 has to be replaced by the concept of people's right to information. Public agencies, at present, are not required to divulge information concerning specific decisions or actions to the public. Working procedures for various purposes in different departments have to be reviewed and made as open as possible. The system needs to be opened up by providing a role for the society. Citizens should be actively involved in planning, monitoring and reviewing periodically. This will help to demystify service delivery and empower citizens by informing them about their rights and what they should expect from the service provider.

Legislation to simplify the existing rules and streamline procedures in the administrative system may be necessary. It should provide new statutory powers for regulations to set and monitor standards for specific public services, fix a time frame, help make consumers aware of standards, provide for compensation when guaranteed standards are not met, improve the complaint redressal procedure and facilitate greater competition, wherever possible, in providing services. The presence of competition can dampen the spread and severity of corruption. Multiple providers of service should be encouraged to enter the public utility arena.

Before attempting legislation as suggested above, each department and public service provider should take the following steps:

1. Survey its customers to understand what problems they face in the transactions with the agency and identify the kinds of information that can minimise these problems.
2. Define the standards which the agencies will maintain and the conditions the customers should fulfil in order to qualify for the services.
3. Specify who can provide additional information or clarification if customers require such information.
4. Announce the remedies and appeal procedures available if consumers are dissatisfied.
5. Display the information and disseminate the same widely and periodically to the public through the media and other forums.*

---

* S.Guhan & Samuel Paul. *Corruption in India:Agenda for Action,* p.161.

Concentration of power in a single department or authority, for example, issuing licences, permits and a variety of certificates like fitness certificate, no objection certificate, community certificate, birth certificate, etc., promotes corruption. This type of corruption can be considerably reduced if the powers for issue of such certificates are dispersed among more than one authority wherever possible. Specific items for such dispersal of powers have to be identified.

Public officials are expected to act as agents for the citizens. An agent who has the power to allocate resources may sell his decisions or services for a personal gain. An element of discretion is inevitable in the exercise of powers by government functionaries in the field in many situations. Care has to be taken to ensure that such exercise of discretion remains within declared norms and guidelines. Working procedures in administration have to ensure that a framework of such norms and guidelines circumscribes all areas of discretion.

Accountability in the present system is hierarchical, with little attention paid to the needs of the clients, namely the citizens. Accountability can be brought about by an arrangement for a critical scrutiny of the connected file by an ombudsman-like authority at the district level and at the state level. Such a facility for a close scrutiny of records by a duly constituted authority outside the department will help prevent arbitrary disposal of matters in a department. Citizens can approach this institution not only to redress their grievances but also to get compensation when harm is done by the department. The ombudsman should be a constitutionally-protected statutory authority and it should follow summary procedures for disposal of complaints. It should not get bogged down in the complex web of legal formalities and procedures. It should be made obligatory to dismiss a public servant if he is proved corrupt, entailing permanent disqualification to hold a public office.

The constitutional safeguards provided in Article 311 of the Constitution and a series of decisions of the Supreme Court have tended to tilt the system in favour of the delinquent civil servant. The intricacy and elaborateness of the procedure for taking disciplinary action against a guilty officer has often drawn interference from courts and this has made it rather difficult to terminate the services of a delinquent civil servant. It is suggested that an amendment may be made to Article 311, adding a new exemption clause to the proviso to Article 311 (2) alongwith the existing three clauses, whereby giving reasonable opportunity may be dispensed with in the case of a civil servant who is proved to be guilty of corruption.

Revolutionary developments in information technology can be put to use for bringing about transparency and accountability in administration by introducing computers in a big way as an integral part of the apparatus of administration. Computer communication network from village to state level may be required to move closer to the citizen. A multipurpose citizen database with unique key number for each citizen may become necessary. The database will have the citizen's name, age, income, land holding, education, ration card number, caste and community and other relevant data required to provide various services expected of the government departments. Interlinking of departments with multipurpose connectivity up to village level has to be taken up in a phased manner, keeping the cost factor in mind. Building the required infrastructure has to be taken up as a long-term strategy. Social information booths with interactive computers can be of much use to reduce corruption. The booths, like STD, ISD, PCO booths, may provide information regarding the procedures for availing various services, eligibility conditions for getting benefits, the format of applications, government orders, the standards, the status of applications, etc. These booths can be manned by individuals and voluntary organizations.

Electronic government is the new buzz word that promises to bring about a new culture in citizen-government interactions and transactions. It also offers immense potential for reduction of corruption at field level. It is reported that Malaysia has electronically linked the government with the tax payers. In India, Andhra Pradesh is taking earnest steps for establishing a digital government that will have flatter organizational hierarchies and more personalised delivery of citizens' services. A citizen can access his electricity bill, water bill, and other related services. The Tamilnadu Government has also, keeping abreast of the innovative information technology, initiated action to set up social information booths, moving towards digital government.

An annual performance appraisal report may be evolved with stress on an objective appraisal of the actual performance of individual public servants during a year. It should be an open system and every government servant should be enabled to know the plus and minus points in his actual performance every year. The reporting system should lend itself to an accurate assessment and officers of honesty and integrity should be recognised through out-of-turn promotions and sanction of additional bonus increments.

The civil servants should be made to file annual returns of their movable and immovable properties with the government and a systematic verification of the correctness of such information should be undertaken periodically by the Vigilance Department. The disproportionate income of the civil servant and of his spouse and children should also be subjected to verification and prompt appropriate action taken against illegal accumulation of wealth as per law.

All said and done, ultimately, the citizens should come forward to eradicate corruption with determination. They should realise that they are entitled to the services as a matter of right from the government and enterprises. A consistent and orchestrated campaign should be pursued by social reformers for educating the people, especially the youth, against corruption at all levels. Citizen groups should be formed to tackle corruption in local areas on specific issues. Unless public action and co-operation are forthcoming, it will be very difficult to eliminate the menace of corruption.

11

CORRUPTION IN ADMINISTRATION
Causes and Consequences

S.N.Sangita

Concept of Corruption

It is not an easy task to define corruption, as it is not a unified phenomenon. There are many forms of corruption with different types of participants, settings, stakes, techniques and cultural legitimacy (Peter M. Ward, 1989: 3). The divergence of corruption is much apparent, if distinction is made between formal, legal and cultural definition of corruption. However, Heidenheimer identified three types of corrupt behaviour definitions-public office centered, market centered and public interest centered (Heidenheiner 1970, in Tevik F. Nas *et al.*, 1986: 109).

Public office centered definitions revolve round the violation of public trust placed in the office. In other words, deviation from bureaucratic norms like rationality, universalism and achievement orientation in meeting responsibilities generates corruption. According to James S. Nye, "Corruption is behaviour which deviates from the normal duties of public role because of private regarding (personal, close, private clique), pecuniary or status; violates rules against the exercise of certain types of private regarding influence. This includes such behaviour as bribery (use of reward to prevent the judgment of a person in a position of trust), nepotism (bestowing of a patronage by reason of ascriptive relationship rather than merit), and, misappropriation (illegal appropriation of public resource for private regarding uses)" (James S. Nye, in Heideheiner, 1970: 566-67).

Market centered corruption refers to the situation in which officials look upon their position as an authority to maximise personal gains by dispensing public benefits. Public interest centered definition stresses the violation of common interest that provides direct or indirect benefits to the public officials. In this paper, public office centered definition of corruption is used. It broadly refers to abuse of public office for personal gain. Corruption in high places or macro level is political corruption while corruption at grassroots or micro level is administrative corruption.

Black money, on account of tax evasion, increased from 700 crores in 1961-62 to 10,000 crore in 1965-66, and, Rs.14,000 crore in 1968-69. However, according to the latest guess estimates, it has gone up to Rs.68,324 crore in 1987-88 from Rs.26,528 crore in 1980-81. Among these, income-tax occupied the first place with Rs.34,329 crore during 1987-88. It was followed by states (Rs.16,131 crore), excise duty (Rs.10.951 crore), customs duty (Rs. 5,953 crore), and corporate tax (Rs.1,030 crore).

Black income from urban real estate, smuggling and government expenditure accounted for around a little less than half of the total black money. Black income due to encroachment and acquisition of valuable urban property and so on was estimated around Rs.5,260 crore in 1980-81 and it was 18,847 in 1987-88. Smuggling money was estimated to be a few hundred crores in 1960s, which rose to Rs.1,200 crore in 1980-81 and Rs.12,000 crore in 1987-88.

The issue of corruption (using public office for personal gain) has attracted public interest in India in recent years. Many scandals involving huge amounts of money in the form of kickbacks and so on in high places are widely discussed in the media and at various fora (parliament, state legislatures, party organizations, and the elections). Many surveys have pointed out that, for every third Indian, corruption is a major problem. Moreover, India is rated as the seventh most corrupt country in the world (Transparency International). The number of public personalities of the country (including Ministers and leaders of political parties) involved in scandals is increasing. Similarly the number of senior administrators, whose names have been associated with unethical activities, has increased over the years. Many instances of scandals, fraud, crime and corruption involving them have came to the light in recent years (Sangita and Vibha, 1996)

Black operations (black money and criminal activities), which are closely associated with political and administrative corruption, are in the ascendency. Black money (unaccounted money, generated through tax evasion, smuggling, encroachment and illegal acquisition of urban real estate and leakages from government expenditure), which constituted 41.71 per cent of the GDP in 80-81, rose to 45.81 per cent in 1983-84 and 51.7 per cent in 1987-88. The growth rate of black money was slightly higher than the GDP during 1980-88 (46.5 per cent for black money and 40 per cent for GDP) (Sangita, 1995).

Leakages from government expenditure are yet another source of black money and corruption. It is believed that 10 to 20 per cent of illicit money is siphoned off from government contracts/purchases. According to Robert Wade, illicit income to the engineers in canal maintenance in a South Indian State in late 1972 was estimated around 25 to 50 per cent. It was 50 to 60 per cent, according to Pant, in the Kosi Canal System in Bihar. Talwar has estimated that 25 to 30 per cent of the recorded costs of public works in Delhi and neighbouring states was siphoned off illicitly by government functionaries, politicians and contractors, while it was as high as 80 per cent in land development, acquisition and other works.

Corruption at the grassroots has become a way of life. In rural areas, nothing moves without speed money in public offices. People are compelled to pay bribes to get government services and facilities (certificates, licences, *katha* transfers, building plan approvals, registration of properties, and admission in schools and hospitals). Approval of substandard works (roads, buildings and earth works) and procurement of poor quality goods (medicines, materials, agricultural inputs and implements) are very common. Stealing of power, water (through unauthorized connections) and essential items (of public distribution system) and encroachment and misuse of government properties are very frequent. Misappropriation of funds meant for rural development and weaker sections is reported widely (according to the late Prime Minister Rajiv Gandhi, only 15 per cent of the development benefit reached the poor).

This is the situation with regard to corruption at both the macro and micro levels, notwithstanding change of governments frequently at both the national and state levels on the issue of corruption and introduction of many anti-corruption strategies. For instance, anti-corruption institutions like the Central Bureau of Investigation (CBI), Central Vigilance Commission, Enforcement Directorate at the national level and *Lokayukta,* Vigilance Commissioner, and Anti-Corruption Bureau CID at the state level have made very limited impact in containing corruption, although judicial activism, independent audit, free press, and legislative bodies have played a significant role in exposing corrupt people in high places in recent years.

On the other hand, many scholars have expressed reservations about the ability of decentralized governing institutions like Panchayati Raj Institutions (PRIs), Non-Governmental Organizations (NGOs) and people's movements to minimize corruption. Notwithstanding these developments, many efforts are on to eradicate corruption in recent years. They include: electoral reform, introduction of Lok Pal Bill, Action Plan for Effective and Responsive Government, Citizen's Charter, Right to Information, and, Electronic Government. The Central Vigilance Commission has taken new initiatives like computerization of banking transactions, banning of post-tender negotiations and transport procedures and manual for public undertakings to control corruption.

The present paper analyses the causes and the cost of corruption in administration with a view to suggesting appropriate strategies to contain corruption in public life. The second section diagnoses the causes of corruption in administration from individual and structural perspective with a view to evolving appropriate anti-corruption strategies. In the third section, the consequences of corruption on polity (legitimacy and capacity to govern), economy (investment and growth), and society (removal of poverty and sustainable environmental and social development) are discussed. The fourth section evaluates the limitations of anti-corruption strategies in terms of institutional strength, political and administrative will and societal support and vigilance.

Causes of Corruption

The causes of corruption are many and they vary across states and departments and within the same state and department at different points of time. For the purpose of clarity, the sources of corruption are viewed from individual and system perspectives. Individual perspective tends to view corruption from individual values, beliefs, perceptions, attitudes, economic status, and, incentive and disincentive mechanisms.

Individual Perspective

Firstly, individuals with high levels of moral development and values are always resistant to the temptation of corruption. For instance, the sacrifices of pre-Independence leaders for the country's freedom and the suffering of administrators (in regard to frequent transfers and promotional blockades) to uphold values and public interest can be mentioned in this regard. On the other hand, persons with materialistic orientation, improper conduct and poor self-discipline cannot withstand the temptations and their greed or desire to gain more money pushes them into corrupt practices. Therefore, motivation and ethical values of administrators are essential to contain corruption.

Secondly, motivation to earn illegal income is strong if the existing inequalities are acute and salaries of public officials are very low.

Thirdly, incentive and disincentive mechanism is also a contributory factor for corruption. Various incentive and disincentive mechanisms are suggested by scholars to control individual level corruption in administration. They are: selection of agents for their honesty and capability by screening out the dishonest, changing the usual bureaucratic pattern of incentives and disincentives by rewarding honesty and integrity, and penalizing corrupt behaviour in a deterrent manner (i.e., take the profit out of corruption), training of officials to inculcate moral standards, promulgation of codes of ethics, changing of organizational culture and so on (Klitgaard, 1988; Caiden, 1993).

Integrity can be safeguarded only if able and virtuous people are attracted to public service and if the compensation is sufficient so that they do not feel obliged to resort to corruption to sustain a standard of living compatible with their status and rank in society (Caiden, 1988:23). Independent auditing and anti-corruption agencies would increase the probability of detection and conviction, thus, raising the psychic costs of corruption. Also screening out the dishonest, frequent transfers, reduction of monopoly power and discretion, removal of privileges and negative publicity and so on can deter officials from undertaking corrupt activities. Legal codes or laws relating to collection of political funds, acceptance of bribes or gifts, disclosure of assets and liabilities, acquisition of property and so on can also regulate the behaviour of public servants.

Fourthly, individual corruption is also determined by the quality of political leadership. Therefore, the leaders should not only maintain high standards in public life but also exhibit strong will to eradicate corruption. According to Caiden, "the first strategic target is political corruption – the end to all dirty tricks in politics and creation of an ethos whereby politicians, political officials and party functionaries are not only fair and honest but also take a dim view of official corruption in any shape or form. Political leaders must be committed to the eradication of corruption by setting a good example themselves."

Fifthly, individual ethical behaviour also depends upon the ethical values of the society. It is argued by some scholars that no anti-corruption strategy is effective unless it is supported by the ethical values of the society. In other words, good governance of a country depends upon the moral character and standards of the people. According to Plato, "people get the government they deserve." This implies that society as a whole accepts certain standards of behaviour regarding fairness and propriety. Corruption thrives when there is no consensus on these standards. An important corrective mechanism then is a common standard of morality (Gillespie and Okruhlk, 1991:81). Moral standards in the society can be achieved by continuous education, particularly moral education through the family, schools, media, peer or social groups (religious organizations), political parties and so on. Through these efforts, society can inculcate a willingness to sacrifice self-interest for the common welfare (Gillespie and Okruhlik, 1991:80; Caiden, 1988:22)

Systems Perspective

System level perspective includes (1) Monopoly or State control, (2) Discretionary power without effective control, (3) Complex and obsolete laws, regulations and procedures, and (4) Political corruption.

Monopoly or State Control: Several studies have assessed the relationship between state controlled economy and the incidence of corrupt activity. In fact, corruption is more in states where state controls are very high. This is the situation in many socialist countries, where excess of state controls has led to rampant corruption. Monopoly rents are very large in these countries. Even the economic rents due to wastages, leakages including corruption in these countries are very high.

Excessive regulation alongwith greater discretionary powers in administration provides opportunities for corruption since regulations can be used to frustrate the public and extort bribes. We found this trend in our findings on the basis of complaints against persons trapped and found guilty by the Anti-Corruption Machinery (ACM) in Karnataka during 1956-95. Corruption due to regulatory controls accounted for the highest percentage of the total number of corruption cases. Corruption pertaining to issuance of certificates, licences and permits occupied the first position in Karnataka. It accounted for around 14.9 per cent. If all the departments are put together, it is more than half in departments like Labour, Food and Civil Supplies, Weights and Measures, Mines, Excise, Forest, Industry, and Animal Husbandry.

The certificates mainly include caste and income certificates, vehicle registration and no-objection certificates and so on. The licences primarily include: driving licence, licence for liquor shops, rice mills, and so on. Permits related to cutting and transportation of trees, collecting stones or undertaking mining activities, plying buses on unauthorized routes, and so on. In fact, licences and permits, according to the Santhanam Committee, fetched 100 to 500 per cent of the face value, if it was sold. Import licences worth Rs.238.24 lakh were obtained by fraud and other types of malpractices. The important strategy is to minimize the government intervention and deregulate the society to the extent possible. At the same time, stringent consumer protection and other laws for maintaining ethics in the private sector are essential.

Discretionary Power without Effective Control : Discretionary powers vested with the political system and administrative organizations can also promote corruption. It is generally believed that "power corrupts and absolute power corrupts absolutely." This can be minimised by dispersal of power to various agencies with checks and balances. Judicial and legislative controls (particularly question hour) can prevent the executive from abusing powers. Similarly, anti-corruption laws, independent investigative and enforcement agencies can also act as checks over the executive. According to Caiden, the avoidance of corruption is implicit in the proper functioning of democratic process, a proper division of power among all branches of government, a constructive opposition in multi-party system and free press (Caiden, 1993:34).

Under-assessment of tax or reduction of tax or penalty, leasing out and selling of government property for low price, in our study in Karnataka, accounted for 3.66 per cent of the total cases in all departments. It was the highest in the Commercial Tax Department (64.70 per cent) followed by Municipalities and Transport with 42.85 per cent and 28.57 per cent respectively. Corruption due to supply of information or provision of records accounted for 6.88 per cent of the total number of corruption cases. However, it was the highest in the Revenue Department. Approving and purchasing of sub-standard works/goods is the mode prevalent in PWD and the Purchase Department. A little less than half in the PWD accounted for this. It is customary in these departments to offer a certain percentage in respect of award of contracts of construction, purchases and sales.

Over-payment for works executed by contractors or goods supplied by dealers accounted for around 7.33 per cent of corruption. Corruption under unlawful activities accounted for 3.21 per cent at the aggregate level. It was the highest in the Police Department (41.37%), followed by Excise with 40 per cent. These departments were entrusted with the responsibility of checking unlawful activities like smuggling, drug-trafficking, black marketing, illicit distillation of liquor and so on.

The best strategy to curb discretionary powers and corruption is to expand the scope of the decision-making process to a wider section of the society. Maximum public access to decision- making minimises the role of middlemen operating between the government and the people. Substantive participation in the political process by all citizens serves to reinforce a sense of civic virtue and prevents government agencies from becoming isolated. In fact, decentralization and democratization of political system through multi-level governments and agencies (State and Local Governments, political parties, NGOs and so on) can involve a larger section of the society in the country's governance and minimise the level of corruption (Sangita, 1993; Smith, 1990).

Discretionary and monopoly power can also be contained by strengthening the information sources (auditors, investigators, whistle-blowers, Ombudsmen, and other anti-corruption bodies) both inside and outside agency (Klitgaard, 1988). Similarly, simple procedures and methods, transparency in administration, periodical transfers and organization of clientele as anti-corruption lobby are also suggested by scholars to curb corruption in the system (Klitgaard, 1988).

Complex and Obsolete Laws: Another contributory factor for corruption is the existence of several bottlenecks in administration. In fact, many existing laws are obsolete and redundant. People bribe the officials to overcome these administrative hurdles. This is more so in departments like Education, Revenue, Bangalore Development Authority, and other urban local bodies, which could be minimised by streamlining the administration with clearcut set of procedures and effective communication. In this regard, certain recommendations of the Andhra Pradesh Lokayukta were quite innovative. For instance, in some cases, where the Lokayukta noticed prevalence of red-tapism and cumbersome procedures and formalities in fixing rent for buildings taken on rent by the government departments, certain reforms for cutting such delays were suggested.

Political Corruption : Political corruption is the main source for administrative corruption. Political corruption mainly includes malpractice in elections, appointments and transfers. Election competition based on money and muscle power is the main source of political corruption. In the absence of well-knit organization and cadre, political parties resort to money power and muscle power (criminal *gangs* come handy for this purpose) to mobilize people. This is evident from reports showing a large percentage of members in Bihar and UP Assemblies with criminal background. Democratization of political parties and introduction of a code of conduct appears to be a viable method of arresting such trends. Electoral reforms, including funding of elections by the government, is also an essential requirement to control political corruption.

Another source of political corruption is appointments and transfers in the government. It is a fact that a certain percentage of postings and transfers are priced. As a result of this, a large section of unemployed youth appear to have lost faith in the impartial conduct of Provincial Public Service Commissions (irrespective of the state). The image of these commissions can be restored by opening their activities to scrutiny by *Lokayukta.* Similarly, initiative has to be taken to control corruption in transfers by evolving an unambiguous transfer policy to avoid frequent transfers. In fact, according to David Potter's study of 1985, the average stay of district level officers in Karnataka was less than a year.

Consequences and Cost of Corruption

Corruption is highly harmful to polity, society and economy. According to many scholars, corruption is harmful to societies and governments, impeding development and eroding the legitimacy of even honest, elite and well-run institutions. Revisionists, by contrast, point to possible access for the excluded and perhaps even produce *de facto* policies more effective than those emerging from legitimate channels.

Political Legitimacy and Sustainability

Firstly, corruption undermines the credibility and legitimacy of the government and thereby its capacity to govern. Parallel governments and economies, non-compliance of government guidelines and regulations (tax evasion, auction of jobs, transfers, promotions, and middlemen between government and people) are some of the symptoms of bad governance. The attraction of youth towards radical movement and violence, low percentage of voter turnout and frequent political instability can be partly attributed to the high incidence of corruption.

Economic Performance

Corruption harms economic performance in many ways. Firstly, corruption reduces economic growth by lowering incentives to investment by both domestic and foreign investors. Empirical evidence based on cross-country comparison does indeed suggest a relation between corruption and investment and economic growth. In corrupt countries, enterprise managers spend a considerable amount of time with public officials. According to a survey on the basis of responses from 3,000 firms in 59 countries, managers spend a greater share of their management time with administrators and public officials negotiating licences, signatures and taxes. The study also suggests that the cost of capital for firms tends to be higher where bribery is more prevalent.

Secondly, economic development is also hampered by poor quality of infrastructure and other services, and decrease in tax revenues as well. The need to lay municipal roads every year and the poor quality of electricity and telephone facilities with frequent breakdowns can be mentioned in this context.

Thirdly, corruption may also harm economic development by distorting the composition of government expenditure. Corrupt politicians may be expected to spend more public resources on those items on which it is easier to extract large bribes and keep them secret. In this regard, the arms deals/purchases of the third world leaders, instead of spending on health and education, can be mentioned. Such instances are cited even in the case of Panchayat Raj leaders, who prefer works wherein personal gain in the form of gifts and bribes is more.

Corruption also causes inequalities in society. In fact, a large per cent of development resources meant for the weak are wasted in the form of leakages and corruption. According to many studies, only 20-40 per cent of the benefits are reaching the poor. In recent years, international agencies like the World Bank, the IMF and the UNDP have clearly indicated the need to contain corruption to ensure faster growth, eradicate poverty and maintain environment sustainability.

Constraints to Containing Corruption

Lack of Political Will

Although political leadership, in general, favoured institutions like Lokayukta to control corruption, yet the genuineness of their feeling in this regard was hardly reflected in their behaviour. This is one of the reasons why similar institutions could not be established at the national level, in spite of several efforts in the last three decades. A similar trend is also evident at the state level, although the institution has been established in half of the states. The state leadership adopted a negative attitude in extending support, whenever, the *Lokayukta* initiated action against them.

For instance, in Maharashtra, the Lokayukta was compelled to recommend placing of a special report in the legislature, when the Chief Minister failed to take action against two of his colleagues who were found guilty by the Lokayukta. Even requests by the Lokyukta to make suitable recommendations in the Act to cover former ministers and civil servants were not heeded. Similarly, in Orissa, the Finance Minister filed a writ petition in the High Court challenging the Lokayukta's jurisdiction to investigate corruption charges against the Minister. In some cases, political leadership not only questioned the *bonafides* of the Lokayukta but also challenged the appointment of the Lokayukta, when notices were issued against them on the basis of complaints. They even restrained the Lokayukta from proceeding further in making investigations against them.

Lack of Administrative Support

In some states, extraordinary delay in sending required information by the state government departments constituted a major irritating factor in the conduct of investigations by the Lokayukta. For instance, in Rajasthan, the departments failed to send the information sought even after repeated reminders. The average delay ranged from two to six years. Similarly, in one particular case in Bihar, the Lokayukta was forced to close a case after eight years as he failed to get the report from the concerned department.

Similar conditions also prevail with respect to cases where senior officers are involved. For instance, in Rajasthan, the Lokayukta's investigation against a super-time scale IAS officer was withdrawn by the state government. In Madhya Pradesh, no action was taken within the stipulated time against the guilty officers, despite the recommendations of the Lokayukta. In some states, the recommendations sent by the Lokayukta were not even acknowledged.

Complexity of Judicial System

The complex system of justice hinders prosecution of officers found guilty. Many recommendations were questioned in the court of law, though we do not have details about the number of such instances. Some of these cases were pending for years together. According to a press report, "Even after ten to eleven years, the officers, on whom the corruption charges were proved by the earlier

Vigilance Commission in Karnataka, were yet to be punished. None of them was jailed. All of them retired from the service. But they kept on appealing in one court after another. The cases are still pending in the High Court. Even if the High Court found them guilty, they will go to Supreme Court. Same thing may happen to the cases recommended by the Lokayukta. Already the Central Administrative Tribunal has stayed in the case of two senior IAS and IFS officers who were suspended by the state government on the basis of Lokayukta recommendations."

The same is the situation in other states also. For instance, in Andhra Pradesh, there were many instances, where the Lokayukta successfully completed investigations against many Senior Civil Servants and former and serving ministers. But the High Court and the Administrative Tribunal came in the way of awarding punishments to them. Most of the cases were admitted in the High Court and the Administrative Tribunal and interim orders were passed, stopping further action in the matter till the disposal of the case. Many such cases are pending before the High Courts.

REFERENCES

Caiden, G. E., "Toward a General Theory of Official Corruption," *Asian Journal of Public Administration,* 10 CD, 1988.

Caiden, G. E., "Dealing with Administrative Corruption," in Cooperation, (ed), *Handbook of Administrative Ethics,* Marcel Ducker, New York, 1993.

Heidenheiner, Arnold J., Political Corruption: Readings in Comparative Analysis, Holt, Rinehart and Winston Inc., New York, 1970.

Klitgaard, R., *Controlling Corruption,* University of California Press, Berkeley, 1991.

Nas, Tevik F., Albert C. Price and Charles I. Weber, "A Policy Oriented Theory of Corruption," *American Political Science Review,* 90(1), 1986.

Quah, Jon S. T., "Corruption in Asia with Special Reference to Singapore: Pattern and Consequences", *Asian Journal of Public Administration,* 1988.

Sangita, S. N., "Institutional Arrangements for Controlling Corruption in Public Life: Karnataka Experience", *Indian Journal of Public Administration,* 41(1), 1995.

Smith B. C., *Decentralization: The Territorial Dimension of the State,* George Allen and Unwin, London, 1985.

Ward, P. M., (ed), *Corruption, Development and Inequality: Soft Touch or Hard Graft?,* Routledge, London, 1989.

"The Lokayuta Institution in Karnataka": A Trend Setter for Three Tier Structure Ombudsman in India," *Indian Journal of Public Administration*, 35(4), 1989.

"Corruption: Some Prescriptions", *Deccan Herald*, 8, February 1993.

"Corruption: Clean-ups in Electoral Politics", *The Hindu*, 26, February , 1995.

"Enron Imbroglio: Negative Politics and Bad Governance", *The Hindu*, 5 September 1995.

"Anti-Corruption Strategies: A Political Scientist's Perspective," *Southern Economist*, 36(18) 1998.

"Politics Riddled with Negative Characteristics," *The Hindu*, 6, October 1998

"Panchayati Raj Experiment in Karnataka," *Kurukshetra*, December 1987.

12

CORRUPTION AT THE GRASSROOTS
The Shades and Shadows

M.P. Boraian, N. Narayanasamy and S. Manivel

Corruption has become an inevitable way of life for the common man in the rural areas. With their distinct features, rural areas, which were once corrupt-free, have now become hot-beds of corruption. Since the introduction and implementation of a plethora of development and welfare schemes with a heavy dose of subsidies, corruption has spread its tentacles over almost all programmes. It is growing at an alarming rate, almost impossible to check. It has grown into a social cancer spreading and corroding the very social and moral fabric of our rural society.

Micro Study

Combating and curbing corruption is a Herculean Task. Steps initiated to stamp out corruption have, by and large, failed to fructify, for such measures were not pursued with the required will, vigour and vitality. Neither systematic nor systemic efforts have ever been made to tackle the evil of corruption at its very roots. Such an effort presupposes an intensive dialogue with the people who are haunted by corruption, finding out the causes of corruption and suggesting practical solutions to eliminate corruption. It is against this backdrop that a micro-level exploratory study has been undertaken in two different rural settings with the prime objective of analyzing the causes of corruption as perceived by the people and the solutions proffered by them for its eradication.

The study purports to highlight the different dimensions and causes of corruption but does not aim at quantifying the magnitude of corruption. Two different villages have been selected for the study in two village Panchayats of two different blocks in Dindigul District. The first one is a mono-caste Harijan village in Ambathurai Village Panchayat of Athoor Block, with a predominance of landless households, where a multitude of welfare measures have been implemented. This setting is anchored by a vibrant youth force operating through a Youth Club.

The second is a mixed-caste village in Agaram Panchayat of Reddiarchatram Block, with *Harijan* households dominating the social structure. With a dynamic and articulate Women's Association, this village has been a recipient of benefits from scores of welfare and development activities.

The selection of these two villages is based on the premises that

- the worst affected by corruption are the socially and economically marginalized community;
- welfare and development programmes with a high proportion of subsidy are a rich source of corruption; and
- organized resistance through Youth Club and/or Women's Association may help mitigation if not total eradication of corruption.

Methodology

Rapid Rural Appraisal method was used in harvesting the views and experience of the villagers. The authors, with a team of staff trained in PRA techniques, interacted with different sections of the community on an individual as well as on small group basis with a checklist on the theme chosen for the study. The purpose was to quickly understand the different dimensions of the problems and to identify the key informants who had been subjected to corruption. This was followed by a focus-group discussion with the key informants and members and office-bearers of the youth club and Women's Association in order to narrow down the focus of the study on to the roots, forms and causes of corruption and evolve appropriate solutions to wipe out corruption from the village scene. The findings of the study are qualitative in nature and adequate care has been taken to eliminate the likely biases which normally surface in such studies.

Shades of Corruption

Corruption, as perceived by the people in the study villages, has several shades. It means:

- a person earning without putting in any labour;
- a person earning from the labour of another person;
- a middleman earning from two persons simultaneously (i.e., the buyer and the seller);
- delaying a work unnecessarily (in anticipation of bribe);
- refusal by officials to discharge their duty;
- executing a public work in a sub-standard manner;
- giving false hopes to the poor regarding benefit from government schemes;
- providing services to officials for performing/discharging their duty;
- compelling the public with restricted options in availing public services; and
- ignoring the most urgent needs of the sick and making them wait in order to get bribe.

People in both the villages pointed out several areas in which corruption breeds. They include:

Housing

* obtaining house site pattas
* getting free housing loans
* repairing of old houses

Ration Card

* application for ration card
* renewal of old ration card

Ration Shop

* quantity of the ration supplied
* quality of the ration materials distributed
* denial and delay of ration services
* outright sale of ration goods to private traders
* irregularities in the entries
* forced sale of unwanted items

Certificates

* obtaining various certificates from a hierarchy of officials in different departments (birth, death, income, community, nationality, etc.)

Electricity

* domestic lighting and repairing
* energising motor pumpsets and repairing
* common festivals and family functions

Government Schemes

* loans
* housing
* milch animals
* machines and tools
* material benefits
* welfare programmes

Police and Court

* freeing the guilty
* penalizing the innocent
* protecting criminals

Government Hospital

* neglecting patients
* expecting money for everything
* merciless and crude treatment of the poor

Process of Corruption

The process of corruption is quite interesting and enlightening.

Corruption indulged in by people in responsible positions or public institutions intended for serving the community is neither an isolated phenomenon nor an unorganized act. Instead, it is ubiquitous in every segment of the society, economy and polity, irrespective of the geography or the culture of the people. The collectorate, the taulk office, the government hospital, private schools, police stations and the court are said to be the hot-beds of corruption. Politicians, bureaucrats, businessmen and brokers are the prime culprits perpetrating this pernicious evil. The Panchayat leaders too are no exception to this practice and they are a recent addition to the list of the corrupt at the grassroot level. Corruption is, therefore, not a casual and haphazard activity but is practised in a systematic and organized manner in every sphere of its operation – be it among politicians, bureaucrats or businessmen. There is a system, a sequence, a share and a size in the process of its practice from the source to the destination.

Corruption is never a one-way process but gets mutually reinforced by the gullible public and the greedy officials in collusion with the brokers. The officials encourage the involvement of these regular middlemen or 'development brokers' so that the bribery is not directly visible to the people and they gain largely from such transactions.

When officials from different government departments visit their respective village level institutions for monitoring or inspection, the people/beneficiaries/consumers are kept at bay by the local officials in order to avoid their interaction with the inspecting officials. Nor do these officials care to contact the community for eliciting their views on the functioning of these institutions – for obvious reasons.

In certain public works rendering quantification or measurement difficult (e.g., earth work in road formation) defrauding by the contractors and collusion by the officials becomes a cake walk. Corruption rarely operates independently and in isolation; instead, it breeds profusely in the presence of a chain of recipients. Under the IRD programme, for example, a series of persons and officials such as the applicants, milch animal owners, brokers, bankers, the BDO office personnel, veterinary doctors, and insurance officials operate this phenomenon in a chain. The corruption chain, therefore, is strongly interlinked and it is rarely broken.

Normally people bribe only when they anticipate a favour or get something free from another person. In respect of government schemes, they consider corruption as a 'service charge', since they give only a portion of the government's money. When a series of individual beneficiaries offer a sum for certain benefits, the officials/ bribe-takers fix a standard norm for such practices. When they do not get the bribe, the officials apply the brake to the process, upon which people fulfil their demands on a warfooting.

While we have saying "corruption breeds corruption," the recent development experiences at the grassroot level, where the government has a galaxy of welfare programmes with free monetary component, suggest that "development schemes breed corruption." Welfare schemes of the government targetted at the poor and the vulnerable, designed to deliver benefits and services either free or subsidized, inevitably serve as the sheet anchor of corruption. Development schemes and corruption are therefore, two sides of the same coin and corruption-free schemes are a rarity.

Corruption has descended on the Village Panchayats ever since they were installed under the 73rd Amendment Act. Barring the entry of contractors, but opening the gates to the Panchayat leaders with power to implement public welfare schemes, has enabled the elected leaders to make the best use of such opportunities. Corruption has truly come down to the grassroots and the local body leaders are perfectly linked to the long chain of corruption from Parliament to Panchayat.

Causes

Corruption is caused by innumerable factors. Any probe involving people or politicians, brokers or businessmen always begins with a mutual accusation of each other. People blame the officials, officials blame the politicians, politicians blame the businessmen, the businessmen blame the brokers and the brokers blame the people. Among the officials, they blame their superiors and subordinates and express inability to break this vicious cycle. Corruption, therefore, is a vicious cycle from which escape is a near impossibility.

Vested interests from the better-off section, wishing to avail themselves of the benefits intended for the poor, liberally bribe the officials for obvious reasons. Such ineligible, better-off bribe givers seize the share of the poor and become richer, whereas, the real poor remain at the same level. Such an enrichment of the non-target groups widens the gap between the poor and the rich and enables the rich to harvest the poor's crop! On the other hand, the officials who manage to gain from both the poor and the rich favour the latter for, their share is then greater.

The community witnessing a substandard execution of a public welfare scheme (construction of overhead tank, for instance) with 100 per cent government assistance and zero contribution from the local people desists from intervening for better execution, lest the work get stopped half-way and that the ultimate losers will be the people and not the government. Whenever, the government gives something free to the poor or a subsidy to the people, it invariably results in corruption.

Similarly, schemes providing assets and assistance to individual families, designed to provide totally free benefits (housing, for example), also face the same fate on account of zero involvement from the beneficiaries, who stand a mute witness to the drama of development schemes, lest they be deprived of such free benefits. Corruption, therefore, is prevalent not only in the public welfare schemes meant for the community but also in poverty-eradication programmes focussing on families or individuals.

Insistence on too many certificates by the government for availing government schemes forces people to bribe the officials in the race for reaping free benefits from the government. The enormity of benefits pumped in on the socially backward people triggers those belonging to the socially forward communities to apply for a lower caste identity by bribing the officials.

Lack of unity among the people, factions and feuds in the village, and the craze for harvesting the benefits of government schemes propel the corrupt officials to extract maximum gains from the vying beneficiaries.

When people want to fight against corruption, but are unable to muster adequate support to win the battle, they fall a prey to the claws of corruption. People motivated to fight against corruption gradually relent and gravitate to the background when they witness the fate of their predecessors who valiantly fought against corruption but tragically lost heavily.

People themselves turn out to be the beneficiaries of corruption when they accept monetary incentives from the politicians for voting. Contractors whose works crumble early silence the people by promising them alternative facilities as compensation. Lured by this, the people compromise on their urge (if any) to expose the fraud.

The thirst of the educated employed for money is the basic cause of corruption. An announcement of vacancies by the government is virtually an announcement for the eligible people to mobilize money to bribe the politicians. The officials secure appointments and struggle for promotions often by bribing the bureaucrats and/or politicians. Consequently, they are compelled to take bribe from their clients as a prime source of compensation. Payment of their share in bribery to their bosses in the hierarchy makes them bold enough not simply to expect but to skilfully extract bribes from the people.

Shadows of Corruption

Corruption casts its shadow on almost the entire society, rarely sparing anyone today. Whereas, the aged of the past had not known them and the adults of yester years had not heard of them, today, even children are well aware of the sources, forms and magnitude of corruption. Corruption, therefore, has got into the vitals of our culture and it is very difficult to remove this vice unless we undertake a dialysis.

The tendency of officials to peel off people's subsidy and the temptation of people to gulp government loans make the officials gain and the people lose, but the government remains callous. Consequently, many a government scheme gets wrecked on the rocks of corruption. Ultimately, this results in enriching the officials but impoverishing the people.

People reported about a contractor who had billed for the road work which was actually completed by the community with the help of college students under an NSS programme. This was possible because of the collusion between the contractor, the Panchayat leaders and the union officials. Lack of information about such irregularities to the community keeps the people in the dark and lack of right to information hampers them from pursuing the matter.

Appalling differences have been noticed in the quality of work executed by the government and the individuals/community with regard to housing. Enormous corruption in the government scheme is the root cause contributing to the poor quality. Further, execution of public welfare schemes for the villagers by more than one person leads to sub-contracting of the work to another person who further sub-contracts. Such sub-contracting of work obviously leads to poor quality of work and multiplication in the magnitude of corruption.

Milch animal owners in one village were reported to administer hormone injections (oxytocin) to their cows or buffaloes on days of sale in the shandy to IRDP beneficiaries. Such animals yielded more milk on this day and a few subsequent days too. But, within a month or two, they were reported to have died. The beneficiaries decried the cheating besides inflicting cruelty on animals leading to their premature death. Perhaps a rethinking is necessary in the design and delivery of government schemes for the poor

People are prepared to pay the bribe after completion of their work but often they are forced to shell out their share in advance. A pregnant woman from a village waiting in an autorickshaw at Dindigul Government Hospital for inability to make 'advance' payment delivered her baby in the autorickshaw itself.

Similarly, a poor family in a village borrowed at usurious interest rates in order to make an 'advance' payment of bribe. A young widow who lost her husband borrowed a sum of Rs.2000 to pay as bribe in order to get the grant of Rs.10,000 given in the event of the bread-winner's death. When she managed to get the benefit after much delay, she realized that the benefits equalled the interest paid already, resulting in no net benefit at all. In respect of a couple of families, the anticipated benefits failed to reach the beneficiaries, and, subsequently, they were pushed into an irredeemable 'debt trap.'

Solutions

The corrupt were reported to be wary of any organized group, articulate persons, the elite or those who are well informed. Creating awareness in people's mind, according to the people, was, therefore, a sure means to curtail corruption. Reacting to questions on the ways and means of containing and curbing the menace of corruption from the midst of people at the grassroots, they offered the following suggestions to serve as deterrents against corruption:

* collective action and protest by victims and the community
* social audit of development schemes at the grassroot level
* empowering the people to monitor any public welfare scheme
* stringent punishment for those indulging in corruption
* officials inspecting village level institutions to elicit people's views and identify their grievances
* government officials not issuing false certificates at people's behest
* people should be bold, courageous and united in fighting corruption
* development brokers/intermediaries should be eliminated
* people should be made aware of the process of all development programmes
* people should be encouraged to directly approach the concerned officials
* community should be involved in the programme implementation process compulsorily
* people should have the right to information and all development transactions should be transparent.

Conclusion

Corruption has penetrated our soil, percolated into our blood, permeated our culture, pervaded our economy, and, thereby, poisoned our polity and polluted our society. Once confined only to the macro level, it has gradually engulfed the micro regions, not sparing even remote villages and backward hamlets from its clutches. With the introduction of Panchayats, the corruption chain connecting the capital and the countryside, the Parliament and the Panchayats, the Prime Minister and the poor is now complete. Emerging from business, transcending to politics, corruption has now descended on development schemes designed for the downtrodden. Development schemes are now making the corrupt more corrupt, adding new layers of corruption, and compelling the common man to become a party to corruption. New shades of corruption therefore have emerged on the rural scene and they have cast their shadow on the grassroots – touching the lives of those who are struggling for their very survival. Corruption has been woven into the very warp and weft of the rural fabric.

13

CONTROLLING CORRUPTION AT THE GRASSROOTS

Lessons from a Decentralized and Participatory Development Administration

B. Mohanan

The media have coined fashionable expressions such as kickback, pay-off, boforing, and scamming, which have replaced old terms like greasing the palm, underhand deals or 'transactions under the table etc. This has moulded the perception of the public that corruption is now regarded as very much an integral, if not inalienable, part of the social fabric and body politic of India. However, it is neither new nor an exclusive Indian phenomenon. Corruption in one form or other is as old as organized human life and it can be seen both in the post-industrial western societies and the post-colonial societies of the rest of the world. Thus, corruption is universal and ubiquitous in nature.

In India, after Independence, several committees and commissions have delved deep into the canker of corruption, identified the causes and unearthed the various forms and incarnations in which it appears. Remedial measures have also been suggested. The most important remedial measure that has been suggested is the establishment of Ombudsmanic institutions at the Union and State levels. Unfortunately, due to one reason or other, an Ombudsman could not get established at the Union level. It is noteworthy that a few State Governments took the initiative and succeeded in creating Ombudsmen at the State level.

In spite of all these attempts at curbing corruption, the hard reality of Indian social life is that the quantum of corruption has been increasing at an alarming rate. Everybody knows that the politician-criminal-bureaucrat nexus is responsible for unleashing the hydra-headed monster called corruption. Everyday Indian newspaper carries news about newer and newer dimensions of criminalization of politics and politicization of criminals.

The politician-criminal-bureaucrat nexus has brought under its clutches the administration of India from top to bottom. However, its activities are graver and more visible at the top than at the bottom Even then I would like to confine myself to a study of corruption at the bottom, since the topic of the workshop is corruption at the Grassroots. The specific objective of this paper is to argue that decentralization of power and people's participation in development administration can control corruption to a great extent. Therefore, the focus of the discussion will be the People's Plan campaign for the Ninth Five Year Plan launched by the Kerala State Planning Board.

Conceptualizing the Context

There is no dearth of conventional literature on the causes of corruption and prescriptions to eradicate it. There are also some non-conventional type of studies that attempt to contextualize and conceptualize corruption. Gunnar Myrdal's study is one of the pioneering works which elaborately analyzed corruption in all its forms. He defined corruption as improper or selfish exercise of power and influence attached to public office or to the special position one occupies in public life (Myrdal 1968: 937). Myrdal made the stunning observation that corruption has increased to such an extent that people have started losing faith in the integrity of public administration (*Ibid*). Myrdal then referred to the folklore of corruption in the whole of South Asia, where people discussed and debated it. Finally such discussions and debates led to public policy formulations including campaign against corruption through government machinery. Myrdal's reference to the 'folklore of corruption' would lead us to observe one interesting aspect of all the discussions and debates about corruption. The brute majority of the discussants must have already indulged in some corrupt activities. Only the fast vanishing rare breed called the true disciples of Mahatma Mohandas, the one who refused to copy the correct answer from his friend's answer script as the teacher instructed him to, could withstand umpteen varieties of lures and temptations around; ordinary mortals cannot.

Thus, in an intellectual discussion, it is also worthwhile to identify the corrupt and their critics. If those who give and those who take and those who do both and balance their conscience between the twin acts are counted out, the residual public would be too small to account for the numerous critics. The majority of the population of critics is evidently distributed among the first three groups; they are, therefore, participant critics. To object while participating is to have a pastime, not to raise a problem. The giver and the taker seem to be made for each other and between them there is a gainful symbiosis (C.A. Perumal, 1998). It is worth mentioning here that a few scholars like Theobald (1989) found corruption a useful phenomenon for development. Valsan, quoting Theobald, refers to the notorious corruption of state legislatures and city authorities by business interests and those seeking franchises for public utilities, which was supposed to have led to the accelerated growth of the American economy in the 1870s and 1880s (Valsan 1998). Similarly, he quotes Myron Weiner also. Weiner felt that "but for the flexibility introduced by *Baksheesh,* India would have been paralyzed with administrative rigidity" (*Ibid*).

Dolly Arora (1993) conceptualized corruption in terms of its relationship to: (i) power and authority; (ii) law and policy; and (iii) the public space. On the basis of the above she has identified three types of corruption, viz., coercive, collusive and non-conjunctive. She has also indicated five major strategies which have been carefully utilized by its beneficiaries to promote and sustain the system of corruption in various contexts. She suggests that efforts at eradicating corruption, to be successful, must address the task of corruption-sustaining contexts and strategies. Even though Arora's conceptualization is within a general framework, it can be found useful to the specific context of the grassroots level. One can discern all the three forms of corruption at the village, taluk and district levels in India.

Political and Bureaucratic Corruption

Police, revenue, excise, motor vehicle, and cooperation departments, cooperative societies and all development departments are susceptible to bureaucratic and political corruption. 'Rush money' for getting quickly what is rightfully due, 'hush money' to escape from the clutches of the law and 'slush money' for big favours and contracts are widely prevalent at the three levels mentioned above. Even educational institutions and administration are not free from bureaucratic and political corruption in the three forms identified earlier.

As is the case with national level and state level elections, all forms of election malpractices such as rigging, buying of votes from the poor and the underprivileged, booth capturing, etc., can be found in local body elections in different parts of India. Making promises for personal favours is widely prevalent at the time of elections. Character assassination of the opponent and mobilizing votes by inciting caste and religious feelings are also nothing but forms of political corruption. Purchasing of independent candidates by offering money and position is widely prevalent if the elected local body is left with no clearcut majority to any group or party. Manipulating the electoral rolls and intimidating voters and other forms of election-related malpractices can be noted in the elections to cooperative societies also. The types of corruption at local government level are often of individual nature involving a client and a bureaucrat or a politician or both. These can occur in the areas of services, taxes, appointments, acquirement or sale of property (Valsan 1998: 374).

Valsan is right when he says that the most fertile area of corruption at local level is public works, including the construction of roads and bridges or sewage systems. The conventional practice of contracting out these works leads to an understanding between the technocrat who makes the estimate of the project and the contractor who undertakes the work. Inflated cost estimation, favouritism in inviting and selecting bids and relaxed supervision of the work with a view to helping the contractor to make more profit out of the work are the standard practices of corruption while formulating and implementing public works at the local level. Often, the contractor is a politician or his relative, often in league with the political leadership of municipal or rural local government. They are likely to be well-connected with the state and central level politicians.

Ever since Independence the politician-bureaucrat-contractor nexus has been pocketing 35 to 40 per cent of the funds earmarked for local level development. Thus, breaking the above nexus is the most important requirement to clean development administration at the grassroots level. How can this be achieved? It is now almost a cliche to say that power corrupts and absolute power corrupts absolutely. However, nobody can deny the fact that it is a universally applicable time-tested dictum. Thus, the remedy lies in decentralization of power and transparency in administration. By decentralization and transparency we mean (i) reforming the political process, (ii) reorienting the governmental machinery, (iii) empowering the citizen, and, (iv) sustaining public pressure for change.

The participatory planning programme launched by the Left Democratic Front Government in Kerala bears the features of the corruption control mechanisms mentioned above. Therefore, in the following section of the paper, the attempt is to assess the features of the People's Plan campaign as a corruption control mechanism. The objective of such an exercise is to understand the extent to which it is a replicable model.

Decentralization of Power

The Government of Kerala has transferred all the developmental functions to the three-tier Panchyati Raj System and to the *Nagarpalikas* as per the provisions of the Kerala Panchayat Raj Act (1994) and Kerala Municipality Act (1994), the conformity Acts to the 73rd and 74th Amendments to the Constitution of India. In continuation of the transfer of developmental functions, local and block level offices of Agriculture, Animal Husbandry, Dairy, Fisheries,Rural Development, Social Welfare, SC&ST

Development, Health, General Education and Public Works Departments have been placed under the control of Gram Panchayats and Block Panchayats respectively. Similarly, local level officers of the above-mentioned departments in Nagarpalikas have been placed under the control of Municipal Councils and Municipal Corporations. This is a revolutionary step in the direction of reforming the political process and restructuring the administrative machinery in the sense that the political control of these line departments at the local and middle level has come into the hands of a democratically elected local government.

Gram Sabha and Groups

The draft list of projects proposed to be included in the annual plan drawn up by the Task Forces and finalized by the Panchayat Samithis/ Municipal Councils/Corporations should be discussed at Gram Sabhas/Ward Conventions. The proposal for projects in each development sector shall be scrutinized by sectoral discussion groups in the Gram Sabhas/Ward Conventions. It is mandatory to have separate discussion groups for SC/ST Development, Women Development and Cooperation.

At the conclusion of the Gram Sabhas/Ward Conventions, development seminars have to be organized by the respective local bodies to discuss the draft plan document, says the order issued by the Government in this connection.

Gram Sabhas/Ward Conventions exclusively for Plan formulation were first held in September and October 1996. It was a grand success due to the simple reason that over 30 lakh people participated in it. People at the local level in Kerala have been given the opportunity to participate in decision making, benefit sharing, implementation and evaluation.

Alongwith Gram Sabha, which is a Ward in a Panchayat, we have to take into account the role of Neighbourhood Groups and Family Groups that operate below the level of Gram Sabha. At the initial round proper discussions take place in the Neighbourhood Groups of 50 families and Family Groups of ten families. A detailed report of the discussions that took place in the Neighbourhood Groups would be placed in the Gram Sabha by the conveners of these groups. These mechanisms have brought in transparency at the very grassroots.

Selection of Beneficiaries

With the decentralization of powers and functions the selection of beneficiaries in most of the schemes is the responsibility of the local bodies. In the case of rural areas, the Gram Panchayat should select the beneficiaries and in urban areas the Municipalities or the Municipal Corporations, as the case may be, should do so. As decentralization implies participatory development, it is imperative that people's participation is realized fully in the identification and selection of beneficiaries of various schemes. It goes without saying that, when people are empowered, there should be a process of self selection based on clear criteria and norms evolved by consensus and applied in a transparent manner. There is absolutely no scope for discretion or patronage.

Fair and open selection of beneficiaries is also a legal necessity. It is the Gram Sabha which has the power to identify beneficiaries. For that purpose a transparent procedure has been prescribed.

In the case of Panchayati Raj institutions, basically, the Gram Sabha will identify the beneficiaries. Since the District Panchayat and the Block Panchayat cannot convene the Gram Sabha, they will get the beneficiaries selected through the respective Gram Panchayats who will carry out the selection process through the Gram Sabha and give the selected list to the Block and District Panchayat for approval. This would mean that the number of beneficiaries to be selected by each Gram Panchayat would have to be determined in advance by the District and Block Panchayats. For determining this number, the District and Block Panchayats have first to lay down objective criteria for selecting the target groups. These criteria would be related to the type of scheme. In the case of beneficiaries to be selected for schemes implemented by the Gram Panchayat, the priority list for each Ward for a particular scheme would be prepared by the Gram Sabha and selection at the Panchayat level based on the criteria for eligibility and prioritization. There shall not be any Ward-wise targets and eligibility will be considered at the level of the Gram Panchayat keeping in view the priority list prepared by the Gram Sabha. However, the Panchayat may, if necessary, determine the upper ceiling of nominations to be prioritized by the Gram Sabha. In no case should the total number of nominations exceed twice the target for the Gram Panchayat as a whole. From the priority list the selection has to be made based on specific criteria of prioritization which are to be laid down in advance. The priority fixed by the Gram Sabha cannot normally be changed for that area.

Determination of Criteria

In the case of Central and State sponsored schemes, eligibility criteria prescribed by the respective scheme guidelines have to be followed. In the case of schemes/projects planned for the different tiers of Panchayats, the eligibility criteria would be determined by that Panchayat as stated in the project approved by the DPC. The Panchayats at each level should also state clearly in writing the prioritization criteria to be followed to shortlist eligible beneficiaries in cases where all the eligible beneficiaries cannot be considered under the scheme. While applying the prioritization criteria the Gram Sabha can fine tune them, going into greater detail into each criterion if required.

Publicity

The criteria both for eligibility and for prioritization should be given widespread publicity. Publicity should be given through elected persons, resource persons of the planning campaign, political parties and their affiliated organizations, voluntary organizations, field staff, etc. A notice clearly indicating the number of schemes, the criteria for each scheme and the number of beneficiaries to be selected should be displayed at the Panchayat office, Village office and concerned office and other prominent places. A separate Notice Board has to be set up in each Ward for this purpose. Pamphlets may also be printed and circulated. Press releases can also be made.

Application Form

For all schemes application forms are to be designed in the local language. The application form should be simple but should contain provisions for incorporating all required details needed for applying the eligibility as well as prioritization criteria. The application form should state these criteria in its Annexure. The application form should be distributed for a fixed period preceding the Gram Sabha and at the Gram Sabha. A common application form for a group of similar schemes can be prepared.

Verification

The application form should contain in it a proforma verification form. The Gram Panchayat should decide on a system of verification either through designated officers or designated sub-committee. Three types of verification are possible. Initially, before the meeting of the Gram Sabha, as many applications as possible should be verified using the arrangements made by the Panchayat. Then, the applications for which verification is not completed and the applications which are received on the spot should be enquired into on the spot in the Gram Sabha by the chairperson of the sub-group and the official nominated for this purpose by the Gram Panchayat. In case factual details are not available during the meeting of the Gram Sabha, the same arrangements made for verification earlier should continue and the facts should be verified. In such cases, the priority list would be prepared by the Gram Sabha subject to the verification report and this should be made amply clear in the Gram Sabha meeting.

Gram Sabha Meeting

Gram Sabha meeting should be called immediately thereafter. Application forms should be distributed at the beginning of the Gram Sabha meeting also. Then the list of applicants from the applications received earlier and on the spot should be drawn up. The eligibility criteria and prioritization criteria should be explained to the Gram Sabha. Thereafter, the Gram Sabha can break up into groups for various sectors and, in the sectoral groups, the prioritization of the applicants can be made. In addition to the criteria determined by the Panchayat, sub-criteria for prioritization to match the local perceptions of eligibility can be made. All the applications should be vetted according to the criteria and the priority list prepared by consensus. If there is no rational method of discrimination, then lots can be drawn if agreed to by everybody. Wherever, Neighbourhood Groups exist, Panchayats can utilize their services for vetting the eligibility of a beneficiary.

In the case of beneficiary-oriented schemes under the Tribal Sub-Plan, selection should not be made in the general Gram Sabha. Special Gram Sabhas consisting of all the tribal families in the Ward should be called and selection made by this general body and tribal families from all the tribal settlements in the ward.

Selection of Beneficiaries

With the prioritized list from each ward, after completing verification of facts, a list based on clear criteria of prioritization should be drawn up for the Gram Panchayat as a whole. This should be drawn up in the Gram Panchayat Committee Meeting. To this special meeting, the local press and the public may be given access.

Once the Gram Panchayat finalizes the list, it shall publish it as a draft in the order of priority and indicating the factors which resulted in the priority rank in a tabular form. If any objections are received aganist the draft list, the Gram Panchayat shall consider them after further verification, if required, and record its views on accepting or rejecting them. Thereafter, the final list shall be published. In the case of Block Panchayats and District Panchayats, Gram Panchayats shall send the final list to them with all the applications and documents related to the selection for taking the final decision. The lists submitted by the Gram Panchayats should be published as drafts by the District and Block Panchayats calling for objection, if any. This should be published simultaneously in the District or Block Panchayats and the concerned Gram Panchayats. Only after clearing the objections should the list be finalized.

Transparency

All the documents like application forms, verification reports, enquiry reports and decisions minutes are public documents which everyone has access to and copies of which everyone can procure. In the next Gram Sabha meeting after the selection, the selected Gram Sabha list concerning that Gram Sabha may be given with adequate justifications. Comments by Gram Sabha may be recorded. If it is proved later that the beneficiary or the enquiring officer or the selecting authority is responsible for an ineligible selection, such person or persons would be liable to reimburse the expenses with interest.

Municipal Bodies

In the case of Municipalities and Municipal Corporations, the procedure prescribed in the case of PRIs would apply *mutatis mutandis*. In the place of Gram Sabhas, Ward Committees would perform the function. In the urban areas the close contacts and homogeneity normally seen in rural areas may not be there. Therefore, the applications for various schemes should be called in advance after giving much publicity as suggested earlier. The Ward Committees, the CDS structures and residents' associations should be given advance intimation of the selection of beneficiaries. Press releases should also be invariably made.

After receipt of all the applications, a detailed verification has to be done of the facts mentioned in the application. Based on this verification report and on the eligibility and prioritization criteria, the Ward Committees should prepare a priority list. The ceiling of nominations for each Ward Committee under each scheme must be prescribed by the Municipal body. In the case of anti-poverty programmes, the specific recommendations of the Area Development Societies should be obtained and placed before the Ward Committee. In the Ward Committee meeting all the eligible applicants should be called and prioritization done in their presence, based on the prioritization criteria and applying the facts revealed in the verification process. Here again, all the records are deemed to be public documents.

Execution of Public Works

Execution of public works is a gold mine for the perpetrators of corruption. As noted elsewhere, 30 to 40 per cent of the development fund invariably goes into the pockets of administrative officials, engineers and contractors. A portion of what has been pocketed by bureaucracy, technocracy and contractor comes to the politician in the form of contribution to party fund and election fund. As part of the participatory planning process, the Government of Kerala issued a number of rules and regulations that could effectively control siphoning off development funds. Among these the most important are the following:

(a) Beneficiary Committees and workers' cooperatives would be given preference over private contractors in the execution of public works.
(b) All the details of public works being executed should be prominently displayed at the work site.
(c) Social audit committees of Gram Sabha/Ward Committee can inspect the work and the documents related to it.

It is an open secret that the engineers take commission at the time of measurement and the bureaucracy at the time of providing advances and of final settlement of bills. New rules and regulations have been issued by the Government, as desired by the Planning Board, relating to cost estimation, technical sanction and administrative sanction of projects, fixing of market rates for the purchase of materials, land acquisition, etc., with a view to ensuring total transparency in construction works. Besides, the social audit system that the People's Plan campaign has incorporated can effectively control the menace of corruption at the time of measurement and passing of bills.

Monitoring Team

A monitoring team has been constituted to assess the progress in the implementation of the project and to ensure quality in the work executed. Representatives of the Gram Panchayat Samithi, beneficiary committee and technical experts are included in the monitoring team. It is prescribed that there should be at least five members in the team. The members of the team are selected by the Gram Panchayat Samithi and the Beneficiary Committee. The monitoring team is entitled to examine the execution of the project. If the team finds that the work is not satisfactory, it can ask the engineer/contractor/convener to take corrective measures. Monitoring is not an evaluation after the completion of the project. It is a kind of people's supervision of public works (See Fig.13.1).

AUDIT

Performance Audit

A performance audit system has been introduced in addition to the statutory audit of local bodies. This is a running audit, which is more corrective and helpful than fault finding, in order to achieve the objective of detecting problems as and when they crop up and solving them. The government established a performance audit authority with the local administration secretary as the state performance audit authority. District level units for Gram Panchayats, Block Panchayats and regional level units for District

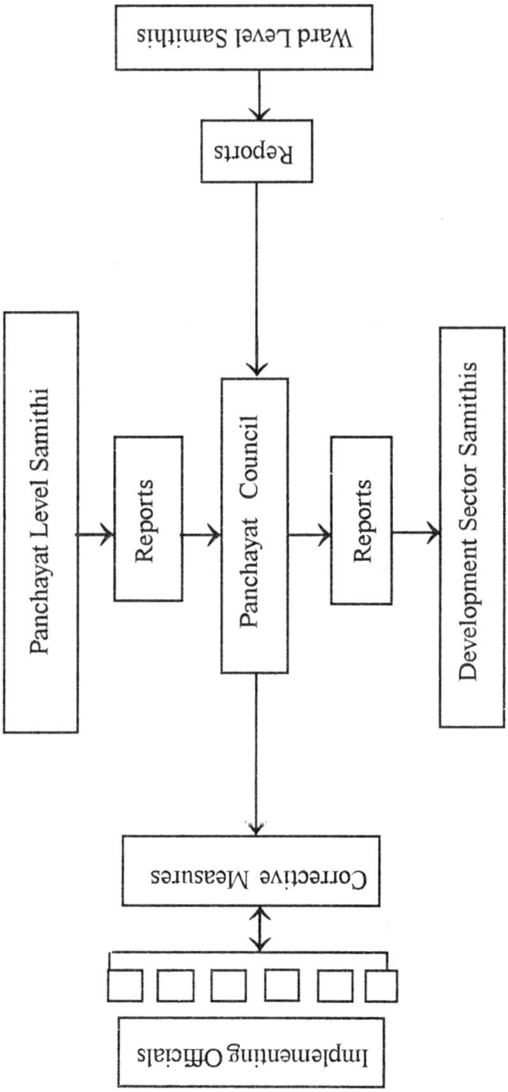

Fig. 13.1 Monitoring Structure

Panchayats, Municipalities and Corporations have been established. The performance audit system would conduct performance audit once in a quarter in each local body.

Statutory Audit

As per the provisions of 215(3) and 295(3) of the Kerala Panchayati Raj Act and Municipality Act respectively, a statutory audit should be conducted annually by the Local Fund Audit Department. The audit party of the Local Fund Audit Department is entitled to visit any local body at any time in the year with or without prior information. They can examine all the records of the local body. Apart from this, there shall be an audit by the Accountant General.

Social Audit

In addition to performance audit, statutory audit and AG's audit, there shall be a unique social audit by the Gram Sabha/Ward Committee. For this purpose, the Gram Sabha/Ward Committee is empowered to get all the relevant details of project implementation. The Gram Sabha, if it deems necessary, can examine the records, reports and other details of project implementation. The Gram Panchayat Samithi can work out the modalities of social audit.

Independent Grievance Redressal System

The government has decided to set up an independent grievance redressal system exclusively for the local bodies. Since it will take some more time to set up the grievance redressal system, the government, as an interim measure, has established a grievance enquiry committee at the district and state levels to enquire into complaints regarding non-adherence to rules and procedures in the implementation of various development schemes by the local bodies.

The district level committee consists of the District Collector, the senior-most non-member of the District Level Expert Committee and the District Planning Officer. This committee is authorized to receive complaints concerning Gram Panchayats, Block Panchayats and Municipalities. The State Level Committee consists of Secretary, Local Administration, Secretary, Planning, and, Member, Decentralized Planning, State Planning Board. This committee will receive complaints concerning District Panchayats and Municipal Corporations.

Both the committees can enquire into complaints using any method deemed appropriate by the committee and shall, as far as practicable, sort out issues through consultation and discussions. Wherever, statutory action is required, these committees should intimate the government.

Technical Audit Panel

A Technical Audit Panel consisting of not more than 15 senior engineering professionals, both governmental and non-governmental, has also been constituted. The professionals would be identified jointly by the Planning and the Local Administration Departments. The members of this panel may be sent individually or in teams to check implementation of public works or to verify complaints. During inspections, these experts would look into the observance of the provisions of public works rules and the governmental instructions issued thereunder with particular reference to the quality of work, ensuring of transparency and avoidance of benami contractors.

Concluding Observations

The above sections have highlighted some of the very important features of the People's Plan campaign launched by the Kerala State Planning Board to ensure people's participation in development planning and administration. To facilitate plan formulation, benefit sharing, implementation and evaluation by the people at the grassroots level, the Government of Kerala has devolved powers to the lower level in an unprecedented manner. As a result, administration at the local level has become totally transparent, as per the new administrative procedures.

Beneficiaries of centrally sponsored schemes, state sponsored schemes and local government sponsored schemes have to be identified by the Gram Sabha and Ward Committee. Clear guidelines have been issued by the government to ensure that the benefits go to the most deserving people. The Panchayat Committee/Municipal Committee or the Ward Members cannot distribute benefits to their political henchmen or kith and kin.

Similarly, existing PWD manuals have been amended properly to plug the loopholes. Now it is difficult for the bureaucrat-technocrat-contractor alliance to swindle public works funds. In most of the rural areas, social audit committees have come into existence to supervise public works if the public works are carried out by a private contractor. Moreover, the Kerala Government has instructed the local bodies that Beneficiary Committees and workers' cooperatives are to be given preference over private contractors in executing public works. It is noteworthy that the technocrat and the bureaucrat cannot collect bribe from a people's committee or workers' cooperative at the time of taking measurement/checking measurement and while passing the bills submitted by them. Since the social audit committees of the Gram Sabha/Ward Committees are very active and vigilant, the local politician also cannot collude with the contractor and the technocrat.

It is clear, therefore, that the novel experiment of the Kerala Government has empowered the people at the grassroots level immensely. The government has devolved powers without any hesitation. In that process, one could see, transparency in administration has become a well-accepted public norm.

Above all, the whole process of the People's Plan campaign is a massive learning process. It includes training at different levels and a large number of people, both urban elite and rural poor, participate at one level or other. It is worth mentioning that, in most of the Gram Sabha meetings, participation of women has been very high. This is due to the campaign programme launched by the State Planning Board with the help of the Kerala Sastra Sahitya Parishad (KSSP).

Finally, the question remains as to what extent the Kerala Model of Administration of Development with corruption controlled is replicable. Here, some very important factors, most of them unique, have to be taken into account. Firstly, it is a question of political will. The leading party of the Left Democratic Front (LDF) Government in Kerala, and the Communist Party of India (Marxist) [CPI(M)], decided to devolve power and introduce transparency in administering development. Other coalition partners had no other way but to follow suit. Secondly, the contribution of a socially committed Voluntary Organization, viz., Kerala Sastra Sahitya Parishad, to carry out effectively the campaign part of the programme, has to be given due weightage. Above all, the social development that Kerala has already achieved provided the required logistical environment for launching the participatory planning process and decentralization of power. One can hardly find any one of the above listed plus points available in other states in India.

Notes

I gratefully acknowledge that I have benefited a lot from several rounds of extensive discussions that I have had with my long-time friend Dr. V. Rajendran Nair, who has been serving the People's Plan Campaign, ever since its launching, as a Key Resource Person (KRP), Member, District Level Expert Committee (DLEC), Trivandrum, and, Member, sub-group on labour relations, State Planning Board. But for his help it would have been difficult for me to procure all the relevant documents from the State Planning Board and the District Planning Committee (DPC). I have undertaken a field visit to Kudappanakunnu and Karakulam Panchayats in Trivandrum District in connection with the writing of this paper. There, I have interacted with several members of the respective Gram Sabhas. This has immensely helped me in formulating my views. However, I am responsible for mistakes, if any, in the interpretations.

1. The fact that Kautilya, Aristotle, Polibius and Confucius paid attention to the phenomenon of corruption in administration and suggested measures to control, if not eliminate, corruption would mean that corruption was prevalent in ancient civilizations also.

Kautilya said: "Just as it is impossible not to taste honey or the poison that finds itself at the tip of the tongue, so it is impossible for government servant not to enjoy at least a bit of the king's revenue." He further observed: "Just as it is impossible to know when a fish moving in water is drinking it, so it is impossible to find out when the government servant incharge of an undertaking misappropriates money." For Aristotle, what 'irritates' people 'is to think that their rulers are stealing their money'. Polibius brought out the difference in the values of Carthage and Rome: "at Carthage, candidates for office practise open bribery, whereas at Rome, death is the penalty for it." Polibius further said: "Whereas, elsewhere it is a rare thing to find a man who keeps his hands off public money, and whose record is clean in this respect, among Romans one rarely comes across a man who has been detected in such conduct." Confucius wrote that an exemplary gentleman is needed to have a clean government.

2. The Santhanam Committee (1962) observed: There is large consensus of opinion that a new tradition of integrity can be established only if the example is set by those who have the ultimate responsibility for the Governance of India, namely the ministers of Central and State Governments. Ministers are necessarily the leaders of the political party which succeeds in obtaining a majority in elections based on adult suffrage. There is a widespread impression that failure of integrity is not uncommon among ministers and that some ministers who have held office during the last 16 years have enriched themselves through nepotism, and have reaped other advantages inconsistent with any notion of purity in public life. The general belief about failure of integrity amongst ministers is as damaging as actual failure. We are convinced that ensuring absolute integrity on the part of ministers at the centre and in the states is an indispensable condition for the establishment of a tradition of purity in public services. The Vohra Committee (1996) reported the existence of a parallel government in India run by a mafia.

3. The first effort was made in the year 1968 by introducing Lokpal and Lok Ayuktha Bills. Due to the dissolution of the Lok Sabha, this Bill lapsed. Since then several unsuccessful attempts were made in 1971, 1977, 1983, 1986, and 1996.

4. Maharashtra, Uttar Pradesh, Rajasthan, Bihar, Karnataka, Andhra Pradesh, Madhya Pradesh, Himachal Pradesh and Kerala have already established Lok Ayukthas. In Kerala, the Governor promulgated an ordinance on 15 November 1998 providing for the establishment of a Lok Ayuktha and two Upalok Ayukthas in the State to probe corruption charges against public men and officials. The law will cover the chief minister, ministers, government servants including IAS officers and public men including office bearers of political parties, trade unions and members of local bodies. The chairmen and the directors of public sector undertakings, office bearers of cooperative societies and functionaries of universities will also come under the ambit of the Lok Ayuktha. The appointments shall be made on the basis of the advice tendered by the chief minister in consultation with the speaker of the assembly and the leader of the opposition. While the Lok Ayuktha will be a person who has held the office of the Judge of the Supreme Court or Chief Justice of a Court, the Upalok Ayuktas will be persons who have been High Court Judges. The Lok Ayukta will have the powers of a civil court in matters such as summoning of witnesses and issue of search warrants. If a public man is found guilty on enquiry, the Lok Ayuktha can direct remedial and punitive measures, including vacation of office by the public man through a declaration submitted through the competent authority. The competent authority will be the Governor in case of the Chief Minister and the MLAs, the Chief Minister in case of ministers and government secretaries and the government in other cases. (*The Hindu*, Thiruvananthapuram, 16 November 1998).

5. According to the Santhanam Committee, the causes of corruption are (i) war time controls and scarcity, post-war flush of money and consequent inflation; (ii) the rapid expansion of

governmental activities in new fields; (iii) decline in real income of salaried classes; and, (iv) growth of monopolies and the rise of the managerial class. The Santhanam Committee reported that two of the major contributory factors for the growth of corruption are, first, the partially acknowledged unwillingness to deal drastically with corrupt and inefficient public servants and, secondly, the protection given to the services in India, which is greater than that available in the more advanced countries.

REFERENCES

Agarwal, U.G. (1988): 'Case for a National Level Ombudsman,' *The Indian Journal of Public Administration,* Vol.XXXIV, 249-65.

Dolly, Arora (1993): 'Conceptualizing the Context: Corruption Reconsidered,' *Indian Journal of Public Administrator,* Vol.XXXIV, 1-19.

Arora, Ramesh and Rajni Goyal,(1995): *Indian Public Administration,* (New Delhi).

Indian Journal of Public Administration (1995): Vol.XXI, Special Number on Ethics in Public Life.

Norman, Lewis (1993): 'The World Ombudsman Community: Aspects and Approaches', *Indian Journal of Public Administration,* Vol.XXXIX, 663-76.

Palmur, Mary (1989): Ombudsman (Lokayukta) in Indian States, *The Indian Journal of Public Administration,* Vol.XXXV, 114-24.

Myrdal, Gunnar (1968): *Asian Drama* Vol-11, (New York: Pantheon).

Proceedings of the Seminar on Ombudsmanic Institutions in India (1998), Department of Public Administration, Madurai Kamaraj University.

Sanghi (1996): Deterring Corruption in Public Purchase: Need for Mandatory Price Negotiation Approach, *Indian Journal of Public Administration,* Vol.XLII, 153-66.

Yardley, David (1995): 'Ombudsman in the United Kingdom', *The Indian Journal of Public Administration,* Vol.XLI, 189-96.

State Planning Board, Government of Kerala, (1998): Various Government Orders Pertaining to Participatory Planning and Decentralisation.

Valsan, E.H. (1998): Professionalism and Ethical Conduct of Public Servants at Local Level' in Sankaran Kutty Nair (ed) (1988), *Society and Politics: Issues and Perspectives,* (Trivandrum: Indian Institute of Police Studies).

Vora Committee Report (Ministry of Home Affairs, Govt. of India).

14

SELF GOVERNANCE, MORAL SENTIMENTS AND SOCIAL DEVICES AS CONSTRAINTS TO CORRUPTION AT GRASSROOTS

V. Ragupathy

Corruption at the grassroots in the development process is positively related to the centralization of political and economic power in a social context where a large section of the society is economically and politically deprived. When people are weak and powerless, they are not in a position to have control over the development process going on around them. So most of the development programmes promoted by government or non-governmental agencies breed a high level of corruption at grassroot level. These programmes, sometimes, instead of empowering people, tend to reduce them to the level of the receivers of alms and it is a morally degenerating process.

When we talk about morality, many of the classical economists and social scientists may protest. But, one of the founders of Classical Economics, Adam Smith, in his mostly forgotten volume *The Theory of Moral Sentiments*, highlighted the importance of moral sentiments in economic science.[1] Is it possible to have a system of self-regulation for the management of the development process at the grassroot level without much control from a central administration? Is it possible for people at the grassroot level to govern themselves? To what extent does the state machinery ensure honesty in the development process at the grassroot level? Is there any moral sentiment left anywhere in the village? Is there any case study available on local regulation of the development process in a reasonably corrupt-free atmosphere? What are the conditions for the emergence of such a corrupt-free self governing system? This paper attempts to answer some of these vital questions against theoretical and empirical background.

Operational Definition

Corruption is a symptom of economic and political concentration of power in a deprived society. In this context corruption has to be defined appropriately. For this paper, corruption at grassroots in the development process is defined as a process of misappropriation of resources and opportunities at the grassroot level in the development process by individuals or groups or institutions by depriving people of their due entitlement by illegal and immoral practices.

Individual Interest and Moral Devices: Theoretical Background

Rational individuals are self-seekers in a modern competitive social and economic order. The classical Prisoner's Dilemma Game Theory explains scientifically the problem faced by a rational individual in the present social context.[2] A rational individual is forced to be a self-seeker. What will happen if every individual is a self-seeker in a free society? Theoretically, individual rationality will result in collective irrationality, particularly in a situation where individuals deal with common goods. This situation is well explained by the advocates of the theory of 'Tragedy of Commons'. Individuals, in their effort to maximise their self-interest, may not mind destroying the very fabric of social life on which economic activities are built.[3] Can the State police the behaviour of every individual? State intervention to regulate the behaviour of every individual is not only prohibitively costly for the state and individual (because of public expenditure) but also practically impossible. More individualism needs more state intervention. "The people's quality of life may be reduced and their material prosperity may be jeopardized."[4]

Particularly, in the development process, how to accommodate individualism in collective good at grassroots level? Can you establish a police station or vigilance inspector in every village to supervise the development programmes? Is there any technological substitute like computerisation? Many options have to be discussed with an open mind. But the basic issues are economical, political and moral. Can we create islands of honesty, integrity and transparency in villages in a corrupt national situation? These are the painful questions to be theoretically answered and supported by empirical evidence. Surprisingly, Adam Smith stressed the role of the church in producing and strengthening morality. Like Gandhi, Adam Smith also had immense faith in the individual's moral sentiments. Like Gandhi, Adam Smith also had faith in the role of religion in the day-to-day economic life. Hume explains the need for 'assurance devices' in the form of moral norms in society and explains how moral norms are internalised and are passed on to successive generations through custom and social education.[5]

Olson, in his logic of collective action, explains the problem of individual behaviour in the context of collective good. To Olson "rational and self interested individuals will not act to achieve their common or group interest."[6] But she admits "certain small groups can provide themselves with collective good without relying on coercion or any positive inducement apart from the collective good itself. This is because in some small groups each of the members or at least some of them will find that his personal gain from having the collective good exceeds the total cost of providing some amount of that collective good."[7] Like Adam Smith, Hume and Olson accept the scope for enlightened self-interest, but Olson restricts the scope only to small groups. This is the biggest gap between the two schools of thought.

To Olson, a small group is a group where the individual actions of any one or more members are noticeable to any other individuals in the group. In such a group, transparency and peer group pressure are the two significant contributors of regulating the behaviour of individuals in tune with the group norms and group interest. In such a context the behaviour of the individuals is noticed and regulated and deviations are socially corrected. This view is supported by

Homan.[8] To him, repeated interaction among people gives rise to 'friendliness' and the associated feelings tend to prompt them to establish informal codes of 'good' behaviour and to assign positive utility to compliance. It is called 'limited group morality – the morals restricted to concrete people with whom one has a close identification.'[9]

The assumption here is that, in small groups at the grassroots level, under certain conditions, enlightened rationality may result in the practice of moral norms in group activities and produce corruption-free situations. In small groups enlightened rationality may be more easily reinforced by moral norms than in large groups.

Decentralization—Is it an Alternative?

After the 73rd Constitutional Amendment Act, interest in the concept of decentralisation as an answer to administrative failure on the part of the government is growing. Few think decentralization is a possible prescription for the diseases of corruption and administrative inefficiency. When Rajiv Gandhi diagnosed the problem of corruption in the development process at the grassroots level, he could visualise a system of decentralization (panchayati raj) as administrative reform in the context of demand for liberalisation and reduction of state structure.

But the exponents of decentralization like Mahatma Gandhi, Acharya Vinoba Bhave and Jayaprakash Narayan looked at it not only as a positive process of empowerment and entitlement, restoration of freedom and liberty in a pure secular sense but also as liberating morally from the trap of self seeking game produced by the modern civilization ultimately.

Decentralization can produce both a secular and a sacred atmosphere for a corruption-free, honest and honourable life situation for common people. Corruption is not merely an administrative problem, but it is largely a denial of the fundamental right of an individual to have a honest life with self-respect.

Unfortunately, in the name of Panchayati Raj, decentralization, development and social welfare, this fundamental right has been greatly undermined. In other words, what we do today in villages in the name of development, is the abuse of the self-respect of the villagers in exchange for monetary benefits. With a lot of hesitation, I have no option but to call this process 'development prostitution'. It is a wellknown bitter truth: in the name of development schemes, government agencies, non-government agencies and local body leaders loot the scarce resources meant for poor people without any shame. This paper is not an attempt to bring out the pitfalls in the Panchayati Raj system in its present form. Some of the problems are highlighted here with the purpose of explaining the reason for its inability to contain corruption and its capacity to breed corruption at the grassroots level.

Panchayati Raj Institutions are trapped into electoral politics and have became purely political institutions. It is treated as an administrative agency by the government to implement its programmes without any real powers to function as "autonomous institutions of self governance." It is basically a fund-receiving agency and not a fund-generating agency. It has no control over the common resources at the grassroots level. It has not been organically integrated into the normal village. The norms and cultural patterns of villages are not properly taken into account while designing the system.

People are not really empowered through the new system as the system is under the control of the administrative machinery. So what we have to day is not real Panchayat but only a fake Panchayat. To reduce corruption, restore honesty in public and social life at the grassroots level and to protect the honour and integrity of the villagers, the system has to be redesigned. While designing institutions of development at the grassroots level, there is a need to study the existing variety of people's institutions functioning with reasonable success in rural areas. Some of these institutions are functioning effectively because of the enlightened rationality of the members, reinforced by sacred sentiments.

Case Studies

Against this background two cases are briefly described here for illustration. These two villages have institutions of self – governance functioning smoothly for more than 40 years. The names of the villages are not recorded here for the simple reason that their system must not be disturbed by government agencies.

Case A

This village is in the eastern part of the Sivagangai district. Agriculture is mainly tank irrigated and there are very few wells. The village is socially homogeneous, consisting mainly of small farmers. A single backward class community, mostly Christians, dominates the affairs of the village. The irrigation tank and the church are the centres of social activity in the village. The village has a village assembly consisting of the heads of the households and the executive committee is elected by the village assembly. The village assembly meets on requirement and not based on any fixed interval. However, it is found from the records that meetings are held at least six times in a year. The tenure of the executive committee is one year.

The village has a fund of Rs.96,000. Out of this Rs.52,000 is deposited in a nationalized bank in a joint account in the name of two members of the executive committee. Around Rs.30,000 has been equally divided among 60 households (Rs.500 for each household) and distributed as a loan for one year at 36 per cent interest. The remaining Rs.14,000 is kept in an Savings Bank account in the local post office in a joint account in the name of the two members of the executive committee. The sources of income to the community fund are monthly contributions from the households, the income from auctioning the fishing rights in the irrigation tank, income from trees in the village common lands, fines and penalties, interest from capital, rent from utensils and chairs, contributions from the households on specific demand by the community for specific purposes and occasional assistance from NGOs.

The major expenditures of the community are annual clearance of the supply channel to the irrigation tank, repair and maintenance of the tank, village festival, annual community lunch, repair and extension of school building, construction of building of public utility, contribution to local library, expenditure on visits of government dignitaries to the village, funeral expenses of poor families and gifts to government officials. The annual expenditure for the year 1996-97 was Rs.84,000. The village assembly has complete control over the accounts of the community fund. Without the knowledge of the assembly the executive committee cannot spend more than five hundred rupees at a time. In case of emergency, the executive committee should consult some important elders in the village to take important decisions.

The irrigation tank in the village is the centre of activity. Strict rules are prescribed on contribution and benefit sharing related to the irrigation tank. In times of scarcity water is equally divided between households having land, irrespective of the size of the land holding. In other words, land may be a private property, but water is a common property in the village, of which all households have equal share. It ensures minimum availability of food to all the households even in years of water scarcity. In the absence of such a norm, the entire crop may fail. The saying in the village is "in the village even destitutes and widows can live with honour and dignity with every right." Goat rearing is strictly prohibited in this village. Liquor and gambling are also prohibited. The villagers took all efforts to transfer a corrupt official incharge of the village ration shop and the organizer of the noon meal centre for the school children.

Income and Expenditure of Village-A for the year 1988-89. Samples from the Records

Income	Rs.
1. Fine for unauthorised use of tank water	50.00
2. Fine for grazing goat in the tank bed (Goat rearing is prohibited in the village)	100.00
3. Interest from the money lent	2500.00
4. From leasing right of cattle grazing in the village common land from three local families (except goats)	1800.00
5. Fine for unauthorised use of tank water	

	from 13 persons at the rate of Rs.50 each	650.00
6.	Income from the rent of utensils and chairs	500.00
7.	Resale of one towel purchased for a dignitary but not used	1.50

Expenditure

1.	Funeral expenditure of a destitute woman	120.00
2.	Expenditure on a trip to the Collector's Office by the members of the executive committee in connection with establishment of ration shop (for two persons)	28.00
3.	Expenditure on purchase of a candle and a match box	1.50
4.	Expenditure on a trip to the Collector's Office to file a petition against the recent resurvey of land by the Revenue Department (for four persons)	23.10
5.	Repair work in the irrigation tank (paid as wages)	48.00
6.	Expenditure on community feeding	640.00

Accounts of the community fund from 1989 till date are found well-maintained and meticulously recorded. The village assembly has full control over the income and expenditure of the community fund. The decisions are taken in the open meetings after discussions and debate. Everything is done in a transparent manner without any secrecy. Records of the income and expenditure are available to everyone for verification. The rules of the organization are locally evolved, simple and flexible. The savings are safely invested in a nationalised bank and in the post office. To generate more income, around 40 per cent of the total capital is lent at high interest (36%) within the village, but by spreading it among 60 households. A close study of the village reveals the capacity of the villagers to run an institution for their development without any outside help or intervention. The process of decision-making is absolutely under community control and there is little scope for misappropriation of resources.

Case B

It is a village in Madurai district in the Vaigai delta. About 50 per cent of the land is irrigated by tank and well. The irrigation tank is linked with the Vaigai Canal and the village is agriculturally prosperous. The village is socially homogeneous and is dominated by one single backward caste. The village has a local community organization in which one single caste plays a crucial role. The village community organization has a community fund of about Rs.30,00,000. The community fund has a history of about 40 years. Major contributions to the fund come from the local common property resources like fishery in the irrigation tank and trees in the village. Other sources of income are reauctioning the government license for a shop of Indian made foreign liquor, interest from the capital, fines and penalties.

Some of the major expenditures from the fund are the festival for the village goddess, cultural programmes, bribe to PWD officials for timely release of water to the irrigation tank, repair and maintenance of the irrigation tank, *kudimaramathu* of the supply channel of the irrigation tank, maintenance and construction of the school building, contributions for the establishment of a Primary Health Centre in the village and gifts to revenue, educational and police officials. The annual income and expenditure come to around five to six lakhs rupees.

The fund is maintained by a village committee. The major portion of the fund is deposited in a nationalized bank in a joint account in the name of the three members. For operational purposes cash is kept in an iron safe in the temple with three different locks. The keys of the locks are distributed among three members of the committee. The accounts of the funds are well maintained by an accountant paid by the community. The decisions on the fund are taken in the community gathering after open discussion.

The system is functioning for the last 38 years without any major problem. The membership of the executive committee is rotated once a year among the households of the village. The village community has two institutions. The village assembly of the heads of the families and the executive committee selected by the village. All important decisions are taken in the village assembly and the committee executes the decisions of the village assembly and looks after day-to-day affairs. The village assembly meets once a year and takes important decisions. In monthly meetings accounts of the income and the expenditure are presented for discussion.

The village fund is popularly controlled. Decisions are taken transparently, accounts are known to everyone, the rules of the organization are simple and flexible, there is no outside agency to regulate the community, the state can not interfere in the affairs of the community and the people are satisfied.

Some of the striking features/similarities found in the cases discussed in this paper, relating to the emergence of a corruption proof situation at the grassroots level in the development process, are listed here.

* The groups are small, the members are known to one another and the behaviour of every individual is closely watched by the other individuals.
* The activities of the group directly affect the life of the members of the group in terms of risk or profit.
* The members of the group are satisfied with the relationship between their contribution and the benefit they get.
* The members of the group easily yield to group pressure.
* The group is autonomous and operates without any outside intervention.
* The business of the group is transparent and accountable.
* The rules are very simple and known to each and every one.
* Norms and rules are evolved by repeated experiments and are flexible to the changing needs.
* The groups are evolved out of felt necessities and out of repeated experiments.
* The groups are linked directly or indirectly with sacred institutions, sacred resources, traditional sentiments and moral

sentiments (Temples, irrigation tanks, grazing lands, trees and fisheries).

* No outsider is permitted to take any important decision.
* No outside agency makes any significant impact on the group process.
* The group activities are predominantly utilitarian, functional and goal-oriented.
* Decisions are taken by a process of consensus and electoral process is avoided.
* As rules and norms are traditionally evolved they are supported by moral sentiments.
* The breakers of the rules are socially detected and socially penalised.
* Exclusion of members from the group is possible.
* Rules are socially enforced.
* Principle of equity exists in the allocation of values by the group.

Co-management—An Approach to Development Process

Decentralization must not stop with the elected leaders of Panchayats. In the name of Panchayats a new set of *Zamindars* must not be created at the village level. In the existing social structure, decentralization has to be carefully fitted to accommodate the interests of the most deprived. Decentralization to the level of the weakest section must be effected and reservation will not serve the purpose. 'Power to people' must be effected by recognizing the need for several types of functional groups working at the operational level. The concept of co-management by empowering user groups, self-help groups, and groups of the socially deprived within the larger framework of the Panchayati Raj System has great scope. Once people are empowered and capacitated, the demand for transparency and accountability will come from below. As discussed earlier, in such a positive social context, the scope for corruption will be reduced.

Conclusion

Moral norms, assurance and social devices as constraints:

"The main role of moral norms is that it leads people to perceive the 'game' of social life as a kind of generalized assurance game."[10] Moral norms have a determining role in social life in the modern context. "Moral norms arise more easily in small than in large groups and tend to represent the collective rational outcome as morally desirable norms of limited morality are easier to come by than those of generalized morality."[11] Moral norms can be socially generated and voluntary cooperation can emerge more readily in small groups than in large groups. In a small group individual has better assurance of the practice of moral norms and he is not exploited for practising the moral norms of the group. Enlightened self-interest and reinforcing moral sentiments are crucial to the stability and progress of social life. The cases discussed here constitute empirical evidence of the scope for the practice of moral norms without compromising the self-interest of individuals. Decentralization will be useful as a device and as a process not only for development but also for restoring the honour of the individual and establishing a positive atmosphere for the emergence of moral norms and clean social and public life.

REFERENCES

1. Smith, Adam, 1759. *The Theory of Moral Sentiments.* Ed. by D.D. Raphael and A.L. Macfie (Indianapolis: Liberty Classics, 1982).
2. Baland, J.M. and J.P. Platteau, 1996. *Halting Degradation of Natural Resources.* (Oxford: Oxford University Press).
3. The criminalization of economic, social and political life in big cities like Mumbai and New Delhi is a great threat to the foundation of civil society. Life in these cities is slowly going into the hold of *mafia gangs.* The State is helplessly watching the collapse of governance and social life.
4. Baland J.M. and J.P. Platteau, *op. cit.*, p.137
5. McNally, 1988. *Political Economy and Rise of Capitalism.* (California: California University Press, pp.168-9).
6. Olson M., 1965. *Logic of Collective Action.* (Cambridge: Harward University Press).

7. *Ibid.*, pp.1-2
8. Homans, G.C., 1950. *The Human Group.* (New York: Harcourt Brace & Co.) p. 5.
9. Baland, J.M. and J.P. Platteau, *op.cit.*, p.122.
10. *Ibid.*, p.119.
11. *Ibid.*, p.119

15

COMBATING CORRUPTION AT GRASSROOTS LEVEL

V.A. VASUDEVARAJU

The dictionary meanings of the word *corruption* are: rottenness, putrid matter, impurity, bribery, widespread moral deterioration, fraud, irregular alteration of a text or language from its original state and decomposition of organic matter. In common usage, corruption denotes bribes received by public servants while performing their functions providing scope for fraudulent activities by the public. Corruption is not a new phenomenon in society. It has been in existence from time immemorial. Ancient works on politics have mentioned it. Kautilya, in his monumental work *Arthasastra,* mentioned various forms of corruption prevalent in his time.

In olden days, corruption was confined to a small section of public servants who were found in between the king and his servants. During those days the functions of the government were limited. All services to the people were provided by caste based occupations. Those who provided the essential services, including 'village protection', were paid by the people and not by the public exchequer. Barter economy and not money economy was in vogue. Life was simple, values were high. Hence, offering gifts, etc., was confined to the 'gentry' in the society, those 'above' the level of the common man.

Causes

In recent times, due to the changing pattern of the government from 'Police State' to 'Welfare State', advent of industrialization, expansion of import-export trade, innumerable forms of welfare and development activities, etc., governmental functions have increased enormously. Centralization has displaced decentralization due to the emergence of parliamentary democracy of the Westminster model. Most functions earlier performed by the people at the 'community level'—grassroots level—have been 'usurped' by the government at the state and national levels and also by the public sector undertakings. As a result, people have become 'dependent' on the government functionaries at the grassroots level even with regard to their 'basic needs' such as drinking water, housing, clothing, education and health.

Changes in 'life style' also have paved the way for increase in corruption. Simple living and high thinking were the dominant values in the past. Virtue, culture and non-violence were the values in the past. Now, money power and muscle power have become dominant in public life. 'Consumerism' has nurtured the greed for money to lead a luxurious life. All these factors have individually and collectively contributed to the growth of corruption in contemporary society.

Lack of security in future, absence of social insurance, high inflation, low income are the reasons for corruption at lower levels. At higher levels, the reasons are desire to enjoy political power indefinitely and to enjoy administrative power in important positions.

Corruption in olden days was sparsely scattered here and there at higher levels or middle levels. At present, it is found to be 'ubiquitous' at all levels, affecting the day-to-day life of the people. It has assumed such 'enormity' that no one can be left untouched by it. It is very difficult for a person with integrity and probity to survive in the present corrupt system.

The existing statutes and institutions to combat corruption in the country are not found to be effective in eliminating corruption at all levels. The slow-moving investigation, prosecution and judicial processes do not have any impact on the corrupt system. Apart from the manpower of anti-corruption agencies being small and meagre, many among them question why the 'small fry' should be punished when the 'big whales' are escaping. Cost-benefit analysis of the existing institutional setup to combat corruption also supports this view.

Political parties mobilise huge sums of money from industry and trade without maintaining any accounts and spend them during elections on mega-publicity and also offer money to the voters. After coming to power, they work to get back the money that was spent and collect more money for future elections. In no developed country such luxurious election campaigns are noticed as we find in the largest democracy of the world – India. Apart from political parties, corruption is also rampant in Trade Unions, Public Sector Undertakings, Cooperative Institutions and also in the Private Corporate Sector, not to speak about the judiciary.

Outdated financial rules and regulations, centralized system for financial clearance, centralized administration, hospitality-seeking audit departments, vested interests in bureaucracy aiming at financially better postings, are some of the basic causes of corruption in the polity. Corruption is now found to be organized and 'institutionalized'. The personnel of an organization join together to practice corruption. Looting the public and sharing the booty is the order of the day.

Modern administrative practices and management procedures are not yet adopted by the British bequeathed administration even after fifty years of Independence. Zero-base budgeting, Performance budgeting, Programme Evaluation Review Technique (PERT) and Critical Path Method (CPM) are still not followed in the implementation of schemes and programmes. Review of schemes is limited to the old style expenditure performance of achieving financial targets with little attention to physical targets.

Most services to satisfy the needs of the public are provided by the State Governments and not by the Central Government or Local Government Institutions. Hence, in matters relating to the day-to-day life of the people, corruption is found to be more in State Government offices than in others.

The social behaviour of the people and their social attitude are also the reasons for corruption. In the marriage market and in general, when people are told about the salary figure of a person, they also ask about the figure of extra income that one earns from the job. There is no stigma attached to this extra income. Informal social sanction of this kind also breeds corruption at all levels of officialdom.

Methodology and Forms of Corruption

There are a number of methods of practice of corruption. Depending upon the methodology, forms of corruption take shape. Big business give donations to political parties and those in powerful positions in trade unions. Kickbacks to get tenders accepted by the governments at higher levels is a common feature. Gifts on birth days and during marriages and functions to politicians and higher officials are open corruption. A fixed percentage of the value of works to be executed is paid to engineers of executing agency and in the Audit and Accounts offices it is in vogue at all places. About 40 per cent of the value of works are covered by this system of sharing the booty. There are also collection points and collection windows in each office where there is scope for corruption. Money is also collected by the brokers and paid to the officials and offices at the end of the day or week.

A percentage of amount is paid before allotment of work and the balance is paid on final settlement of bill to the officials. Syndicates and cartels are formed by the tenderers to get the works at higher amounts. Subsequently, the financial executor of the works gives a share of the booty to his colleagues in the cartel.

Officials collect payment for issuing free supply forms, caste and income certificates, licences, sanction of loans, providing electricity and water supply connections, making low assessment of taxes, issuing permits, etc. In these transactions brokers play a dominating and determining role. Any one who does not go through the broker is tossed from pillar to post. Even while remitting the monthly electricity bill, 5 or 10 rupees are demanded at the collection counter. To give new phone connections, to set right the defective phone, money is demanded. Thus, corruption is noticed not only in regard to showing undue favours but also while performing normal duties for which the officials draw salary.

Monthly mamool to police stations, Labour Officers, Health and Sanitary Inspectors and Transport officials and Excise officials has become part and parcel of the social life. In addition, good harvests are reaped during Deepawali and Pongal season collections, etc., launched by the staff of the departments serving the public, in a collective manner. The staff spend more time on such collection drives during working hours and days than on performance of their duties.

The visits of ministers and higher officials to the towns and villages also provide opportunity for collecting money to meet the hospitality expenses, in which a good amount is pocketed by the official who collects the amount, of course, with a good share to the higher ups.

Corruption in an organized manner is practised even with regard to free supply of drinking water, house site pattas, *sarees* and *dothies* and in the bulk purchase of TVs, *chappals*, etc., by the government for supply to the villages. In Madurai, the mafia group belonging to a political party was making money in crores by collecting a fixed contribution from each poor family for getting drinking water from municipal lorries for each week. After elections to the corporation Mrs. Leelavathy, the progressive and service-minded woman councillor, opposed this nefarious practice of exploitation of the poor and brought to an end the extortion of money by the anti-social elements. She was murdered by the mafia group in daylight for eliminating corruption affecting the poor. Many like her have laid down their lives to eradicate corruption at various places in the country.

Teachers and doctors are not free from corruption, the para-medical staff too. For awarding 5 marks more Rs.1000 is collected in public examinations at plus two level. Above 85 per cent, for each mark Rs.1000 is charged. Among para-medical staff in government health centres, field research reveals that for male birth Rs.200 is collected; for female birth, the family has to pay Rs.100; for providing a Glucose bottle, Rs.30 is collected; for an injection Rs.5 is charged; for cleaning the baby after birth Rs.10 is charged. One can imagine the pathetic lot of the poor mothers who have no income at times of birth in such government health centres. These are some of the virulent forms of corruption prevalent at the grassroots level making life miserable for the poor.

Consequences of Corruption

After nation-wide tours and on the spot observation of the situation, the late Prime Minister Mr. Rajiv Gandhi stated that, in all schemes aimed at poverty-alleviation and other development schemes meant for the poor and rural areas, 85 per cent is taken by the brokers and officials and only 15 per cent reaches the deserving beneficiaries. With this kind of implementation of poverty alleviation schemes, it will take centuries to eliminate poverty. The expected increase in national production and satisfaction of basic needs as well as increase in family income cannot be achieved by such implementation of schemes.

In Economics, the Gresham Law states: 'Bad money drives out of circulation good money.' In a corrupt setup, good officials and honest officials cannot survive and the poor people are grossly exploited.

In a corrupt political system, political leadership at different levels does not consist of the best brains in the country. Honest and efficient persons shun politics. Second and third rate persons with support of money power and muscle power dominate the political scene. Good policies and good programmes cannot be formulated by them. Dynastic rulers, family rulers and one person rulers emerge, surrounded by a coterie around them. The quality of democratic governance deteriorates. Dictatorial personalities become the rulers. This creates an authoritarian system with the bad consequences of militancy, terrorism and divisive forces in the country. Unity and harmony of the country are in danger. Managing militancy and terrorism becomes the priority of the government instead of implementing development schemes. Just like wasting public money on wars, huge expenditure is incurred on measures to contain terrorism and militancy.

Corruption makes the administration secretive. Transparency and openness of the administration are lost. Neutrality of the civil services is the first casualty in auctioning mega projects. This is prevalent in all countries in all political systems. This category of corruption does not affect the common man in his daily life. At the district, block and village levels, corruption affects all aspects of life of the common man. Of late centralized purchases made by the state government departments to cater to the village needs and block needs have begun to affect the village and citizens, especially the poor. Schemes meant for improving the lot of the poor are the new bonanza to the corrupt politicians at the State level in India.

A vast majority of the people in the country, particularly in rural areas, are still not corrupt and they cannot afford to support corruption. This majority want corruption to be eliminated. They are prepared to support a drive against corruption in all spheres. This provides the rationale for evolving strategies to eliminate corruption at grassroots level in the country.

There are 5,67,169 villages in India. About 75 per cent of the nearly 100 crores population live in villages. Hence, the manpower of the anti-corruption agencies is inadequate to deal with corruption prevalent at the grassroots level. It is also not possible to eliminate corruption by prosecution and punishment. There is an urgent need for non-orthodox and non-conventional measures to put an end to corruption in villages. Preventive measures rather than punitive action have to be taken to free people from corruption. Elimination of corruption has to assume the shape of a mass movement in the country. A strategy has to be evolved to fight corruption at grassroots level with public participation. How could this be initiated? India lives in its villages. If corruption dies in villages it will die in the country too.

The strategy consists of three components: (1) Policy (2) Plan of action, and, (3) Tactics for implementation with a devising advantage. These three aspects deserve equal importance in eliminating corruption at grassroots level.

Policy

In the governance of the country centralization should give place to decentralization. What the village can do should not be done by the block administration. What the block can do should not be done by the district administration. What the district can do should not be done by the State Government. What the State can do should not be done by the Central Government. Village Government has to be recognized and strengthened. The last tier of the five-tier governmental system should be respected by the other four higher tiers of government. The State Government has to shed much of its obesity in formulating and implementing welfare and development schemes for the benefit of the villages and rural masses. The State government should only issue guidelines, advice and suggestions to the village governments. Village Governments should have the autonomy to formulate and implement schemes according to their priority.

This system of government is provided for in the 73rd and 74th Amendments to the Constitution which came into force in April 1993. Panchayats and Municipalities are 'Institutions of Self-Government' as mentioned in these two amendments. Hence, it is unconstitutional for State Governments to treat them as agencies. Once this policy which is in consonance with the Constitution is accepted, the plan of action for eliminating corruption at grassroots level can be designed and implemented by the Village, Block and District Government. NGOs functioning in villages and the village population have to be fully involved in the activities of the Panchayats.

The following orders have to be issued by the State Government to eliminate diarchy and corruption at the grassroots level:

All the staff of the Revenue and Police Departments may be transferred to the panchayats at Village, Block and District levels, alongwith the budget allocation for their salaries to ensure that they are under the administrative control of Panchayats. The District, Block and Village government shall be headed only by the elected representatives of the people and not by officials. At the village level, all certificates issued by village revenue officials in respect of caste, income, etc. have to be countersigned by the ward member and the President of Village Panchayat.

The tender system and quotation system have bred corruption at grassroots level. These outdated procedures have to be discarded.

All administrative, technical and financial controls have to be delegated to the respective Panchayats. All purchase shall be made only by Panchayats to satisfy their needs and not by the higher level authorities in the department. Works have to be executed with estimates prepared at Panchayat level and not by the departments. Estimates of work and expenditure incurred daily have to be displayed on the notice boards of Panchayats. All records and registers of the Panchayats should be open to public scrutiny at all times.

Selection of beneficiaries under the poverty-alleviation schemes and other development schemes have to be done in open Gram Sabha meetings and not in any committee sitting indoors. The eligibility criteria have to be well explained to the Gram Sabha before selection commences. Anti-corruption groups have to be formed in the villages consisting of Youth, Women and NGO representatives who are not on the pay roll of Panchayats or government and are not members and presidents of Panchayats.

All the government departments have to prescribe the period of time for sending replies to the public and also for disposal of applications. The office should issue a token to the applicant showing typed serial number of the application received and also indicate when the application will be disposed of. For any 'quick service' the department may fix a fee. A cheque or revenue stamp for the same may be attached to the application, in respect of which the office concerned has no discretion to delay it.

The Panchayats have to supply materials and tools. The Ward Member and the public of his ward will execute the works either by their own labour or meeting the cost of labour employed by them. Engineers have only to provide technical assistance to the people who are incharge of executing the works. All house tax assessments, and other taxes levied should be kept open for scrutiny by the public.

The police should work under the Panchayats. Any person arrested by the police should be taken for interrogation only with the approval of the Panchayat President and the concerned ward member and these public representatives should have the power to visit and talk to the person in custody at any time. In addition to eliminating corruption, this procedure will ensure human rights.

Election-eve corruption should be checked by the Anti-Corruption Groups in villages. Corrupt officials at village level have to be subjected to social boycott. Milk vendors, washermen, barbers, cobblers should refuse to offer their services to such corrupt officials and politicians. This should be organized by the Anti-Corruption Groups which should function as 'combat forces' against corruption at all levels.

A 'Complaint Book' should be maintained by the village Panchayat in which a citizen of the village can record his complaint against any official/office or politician who has not disposed of his complaint/applications. The Panchayat chief or ward member should have powers to question the office/official who delays action and then take up the issue with their superiors. If necessary, Public Interest Litigation may be resorted to by Panchayats. Corrupt officials indentified by the Panchayats should be transferred or suspended from service by the departments.

Local colleges, universities and NGOs may carry out 'research on corruption' in the local area and educate the people on the forms of corruption prevalent and also on the measures that should be taken to combat it with public participation. To eliminate corruption in NGOs and Voluntary Agencies, the fund sanctioning authorities may sanction a professional consultancy fee of 5 to 10 per cent of the project cost. NGO work should be subject to monitoring by the Panchayats. All activities carried out by departments or any other agencies in the village have to be commenced after consultation with the Panchayats.

People's committees with women and youth and without Panchayat chief or members have to be set up in villages to monitor the functioning of schools, health centres, libraries, and cooperatives to ensure their proper functioning. People have to be educated on corruption; organized aganist corruption and agitations to combat corruption should be launched at grassroots as well as higher levels.

Some of the schemes implemented by the government in which there is scope for corruption were handled by the author of this paper. Preventive methods and procedures were introduced in implementing these schemes during 1991, which were popular among the public. The details are given here.

Supply of Diet Articles

There were about 1400 *Anganwadis, Balwadis* and other Social Welfare Institutions. The value of diet articles supplied was about Rs.2 crore in a year. Previously tenders were called for and the lowest tenderer was selected to supply the diet articles. In 1991 the tender system was abolished. The women groups formed under the scheme "Development of Women and Children in Rural Areas," popularly known as DWCRA groups, were given the responsibility of supplying the diet articles to the *anganwadis,* etc., in their area at the prices at which each item was sold by the wholesale cooperative stores and the bills were settled twice in a month to avoid financial problems to the DWCRA groups. No financial assistance was provided to the DWCRA groups. This provided self-employment opportunities to about 1500 poor women. All defects noticed in the tender system were abolished. It satisfied all Anganwadi workers and the public. Miss. Bhatt, founder of SEWA in Ahmedabad, Magasasay Award winner, who made field visits and talked to the DWCRA members and the public, admired this unique experiment.

Disbursement of Oldage Pension

For about 20 years, till 1991, the old age pension was sent to about fifteen thousand beneficiaries by money order. Under this system, old people were disbursed pension only once or twice in a year. It was learnt that, using political influence, even young women were getting old age pension. To facilitate the old people getting their pension every month, the tenth of each month was declared as the Old Age Pension Day. Instead of sending the pension amount by money order, it was disbursed by the *Anganwadi* workers, each of whom serves one thousand population and who are near to the people. This new procedure put an end to all malpractices. Of course, it was not liked by the politicians at the time of mooting the proposal.

During the Legislative Assembly session, all MLAs belonging to all political parties opposed the new procedure of disbursement of old age pension by the *Anganwadi* workers, who are not government servants. They wanted the money order system only. However, the new system was brought into force. Wherever, the MLAs and Ministers went, the people appreciated the government for implementing the new procedure. The politicians who opposed the new procedure are now disbursing the old age pension by going to *Anganwadis* and the photos appear in daily newspapers every time they do it.

Supply of Food in Welfare Department Students Hostels

The students hostels run by the Social Welfare and Adi Dravidar Welfare Departments were getting the diet-articles from the tender system suppliers. There was pilferage in this process. It was changed. The DWCRA women groups were given the responsibility to supply breakfast and meals to the hostel inmates. The students were happy about the quality of food and the women got self-employment opportunities.

Supply of Free *Sarees* and *Dhothies*

About fifteen thousand people were to be supplied free *dhothies* and *sarees* costing around Rs.3 crore. At the time of calling for tenders, cloth specifications were mentioned. After the tenders were received with samples, the samples were sent to the Indian Institute of Handloom Technology for testing and reporting their quality as per the specifications. Only those tenders which satisfied the specified standards were accepted. The others were rejected.

Among the accepted tenders, the selection was made by a committee sitting in a big room and all officers of the department observed the proceedings and they were allowed to express their opinion about the views expressed by committee members. Finally the selections were made keeping in view the villagers' taste and preference.

At the time of supply of clothes, the suppliers were asked to supply in bundles of 500 numbers each. On receipt of the goods, random sample was taken from each bundle. The bundles were numbered, closed and sealed. The samples were sent to the Indian Institute of Handlooom Technology for testing. Only those bundles were accepted whose random sample was cleared by the Institute. The others were rejected. This process was repeated till the last bundle was supplied and accepted.

The department was instructed to settle the bills within a week of accepting the supplies or even before. The MLAs and others who visited the villages came back and informed that the people were happy about the quality of the clothes supplied by the government. However, the Chief Minister was not satisfied and he ordered an enquiry into the purchases. The CBI, after the preliminary enquiry, only found fault with the government for entrusting this unnecessary work to them.

Fancy Numbers to Cars

There was competition to get fancy numbers for cars. Politicians in power and their Personal Assistants were making the best use of it.

It was decided that only on payment of a fee of Rs.1000 one can get a fancy number. It can be reserved in advance also. As a result, political recommendations disappeared. The government got additional income.

Instead of depositing this income in the general kitty of the government, it was deposited in the Chief Minister's Relief Fund for satisfying the needs of the sick, handicapped, etc., who are in distress. Adequate funds were not provided for Social Welfare under Economic Reforms policy. This was compensated by depositing the fancy number fee in the Chief Minister's Relief Fund. On some days, even Rs.75,000 was deposited in the CM's Welfare Fund from the fancy number fees.

16

PANCHAYATI RAJ INSTITUTIONS AND WOMEN

Means of Mitigating Corruption

K. Subha

This note is based on a few assumptions/propositions, namely:

* Women are more honest, committed, sincere, dedicated and God-fearing than their male counterparts.
* With the advent of the PRIs, it is hoped that they can serve as an instrument for reducing corruption, provided they are properly trained, including training in ethics in administration.
* With increasing decentralization of powers and functions, there is likelihood of corruption becoming widespread.

Democratic decentralization as a political concept aims at widening the areas of people's participation, authority and autonomy, implying larger and closer association of the people with their own government. India's commitment to democracy, development and decentralization is embodied in the Panchayati Raj Institutions (PRIs). The 73rd Amendment has provided constitutional sanction, given a new status to PRIs and has imparted permanency to PRIs.

The historic Bill was introduced by the Karnataka Government in the Legislative Assembly on 1st April 1993 to replace the existing enactment. It was passed on April 7. The Legislative Council unanimously passed the Bill on April 13 and it came into force from 18th May 1993. The Act establishes a three-tier Panchayati Raj System in the State with the elected bodies at *gram, taluk* and district levels for greater participation of the people and more effective implementation of rural development programmes in the state.

Among the salient features of the Act, it is worth noting that the Act establishes a three-tier Panchayat system in the state based on the population as ascertained at the last preceding census, of which the figures have been published. It envisages elected bodies at all the three levels; it provides for reservation of seats in favour of scheduled castes and scheduled tribes in proportion to their population and for reservation of one-third of the seats for women at all levels; and it also provides for reservation of seats and offices of chairpersons at all levels for persons belonging to backward classes, scheduled castes, scheduled tribes and women.

All the three tiers will have an *Adhyaksha* and *Upadhyaksha* elected from among the members. The Panchayat will constitute standing committees to perform its various functions. The Gram Sabha, a concept dating back to the Vijayanagar Empire, is a statutory body today. It is obligatory on its part to convene a meeting at least once in six months. All the adults who are in the voters' list of the village are the members of Gram Sabha.

A Gram Panchayat will be constituted for a population of not less than 5000 and not more than 7000 in an area or group of villages. It will be considered a Panchayat area and there will be one member for every 400 people. For each taluk there shall be a taluk Panchayat consisting of legislators of the state and centre, one-fifth of the *Gram Panchayat Adhyakshas* in the taluk by rotation selected by lottery for one year, and one representative for every 10,000 population. Each district will have a Zilla Panchayat consisting of the members of the central and state legislatures from within the district, the Adhyakshas of taulk Panchayats in the district and elected members in the proportion of one member for 40,000 population.

Election occupies the most central place in any modern political system. The State Election Commission was appointed. Elections to the 5640 Gram Panchayats were conducted on 29 December 1993 and to the 175 Taluk Panchayats and 20 Zilla Panchayats in March 1995. Karnataka thus, became the first state to bring the Panchayati Raj Legislation in line with the Central Act and to hold elections to the Panchayats under the new Act. For the first time a large number of women were elected to the rural local bodies. At the national level, a total of 9,88,106 (35.9%) women have got elected as Gram Panchayat representatives; 59,688 women (40%) have been elected as Taluk Panchayat members; and, 6,106 (39%) women have been elected as Zilla Panchayat members. However, Karnatakata has the distinction of having the highest number of women elected at all levels – 37,689 (46.7%) for Gram Panchayat, 1,343 (40.2%) for Taluk Panchayat and 335 (36.45%) for the Zilla Panchayat. Karnataka also has an all-Women Panchayat in Mydolalu Village in Bhadravati taluk of Shimoga District. All the members have been elected for the first time and have had no previous experience. This village is now considered a model village and the locals admit that the work of this Panchayat is better than that of the mixed Panchayats.

This was a significant development as equality in all spheres is inseparable from active political participation. Further, national development will be more effective if every citizen irrespective of being a man or woman has equal share in all activities.

Women are thus, getting involved in the local political process. They are involved in carrying out tasks in all facets of communal services, amenities and administration, which are complex. One of the important issues plaguing the country is widespread corruption. It is in politics and administration that corruption is most prevalent. This could be attributed to the compulsions of democracy. Elections involve huge sums of money. The amount of money to be invested in elections is very huge. The candidate requires money to invest and later on expects substantial returns on this investment. Corruption is the answer and the status provides the scope. Corruption has assumed such monstrous proportions that India has been considered one of the 10 most corrupt countries in the world by credible international observers.

The time has come to work towards curbing such undesirable culture and 'social pathology'. Corruption is a societal dysfunction and dealing with it has become a part of daily life. The nexus between politics and corruption is the strongest and is not new. Women are no exception to this. They too are deeply affected by it, be it opposing corruption or accepting corruption. Being new entrants to the political field, they find it difficult to face it or they try to challenge it. Women could play a major role in bringing it under control if not in eradicating it. A strong political will and sensitivity to the people's needs and accountability are important elements.

Grassroot level is no exception to corruption, nepotism and malpractices. PRIs are not above corruption. Studies reveal that, during elections, there were many malpractices. The political parties do not follow any standard nor do they maintain records. Money and muscle still rule the elections. This is an extremely difficult situation for women to enter politics in.

To curb this, local electoral system has to be further reformed so that money and muscle power are eradicated. An Ombudsmanic institution could be introduced so that there is direct link between citizens and the local body thereby reducing the role of middlemen. Good governance of the country depends upon the character of the people. A high moral standard is important as a corrective mechanism. This can be achieved through appropriate education, and socialization in core values of life. Leaders should maintain high standards in public life and should be committed to the eradication of corruption.

Corruption can be reduced by wider participation of the people in decision-making. This reduces the role of middlemen operating between the government and the people. Participation in the political process will inculcate a sense of civic virtue and prevent government agencies from becoming isolated. Decentralization involves larger sections of the society in government administration and minimizes the level of corruption. The quality of political participation is crucial. The electoral system, which is based on money power, should be changed. Electoral reform is the major key. However, the system by itself has a crucial role to play. Transparency in government functions, effective electoral machinery, and, above all, a sensitive and responsive public together matter the most.

State funding of elections by creation of a separate election fund is a possibility. This would provide opportunity for women who do not belong to any political party but wish to contest as independents to gain political office without depending on others for money. Also a ceiling on election expenses and maintaining accounts of expenditure can bring down corruption. Corruption corrodes institutions, norms and values. Corrective mechanisms have to be evolved to control or prevent corruption.

Education can contribute to developing a more progressive outlook. Men and women should work in unison to develop society and to give a better status to women. Last, but not the least, is the question of application of the philosophy and principles of social audit to PRIs. Since Panchayati Raj deals with matters of everyday life, there is much talk about the transparency, accountability and responsiveness of administration in PRIs. The present audit system is not working to the desirable extent. The need, therefore, is for an audit that can evaluate the performance of an organization in relation to its goals. Social audit is being seen as a way of measuring, understanding, reporting and ultimately improving an organization's social and ethical performance. It should not be forgotten that women are the major stakeholders, especially at the grassroots. Now, the question is how to apply social audit methodology to strengthen the system: whether Gram Sabha can be an appropriate forum for social auditing or we have to think of another mechanism wherein women become major role players.

In Karnataka the Gram Panchayats have successfully completed their five year term and elections are round the corner. But we have been reading and hearing from local newspapers and other media varied stories of corruption, underhand dealings, misappropriation and mishandling of funds, mis-identification of beneficiaries and cases of expediting payment and greasing the palm. Since women are new entrants, they are likely to succumb to the system, if necessary measures are not taken. There is apprehension that, in the absence of correctives, women are likely to become more dangerous than their male counterparts in PRIs rather than becoming instruments to lessen corruption.

The 73rd Constitutional Amendment and the women's movement have led to motivating a large number of women candidates to contest the local elections. This can be considered the greatest step towards women's empowerment. But statutory representation is only the first step in promoting political participation by facilitating the presence of women. Studies show that women are yet to be mobilized and that, in the absence of awareness, it is illogical to expect the local leaders to adopt aggressive postures and articulate their rights and demands in an effective manner. The need for training and orientation has, therefore, become urgent and necessary, specially in view of the socio-economic conditions of women. Emphasis should be laid on ethics in Panchayati Raj administration. Training of women is also important as an investment in human resource development.

It is evident that there is a need to raise the consciousness of women so that they generate the power necessary to bring about positive changes. They have to be mobilized as a political force so that they challenge oppressive forces. Women especially have to be trained to be different kind of leaders from the leaders that political parties usually throw up.

17

CORRUPTION AT MICRO LEVEL AND WAYS TO CONTAIN

G. PALANITHURAI

Introduction

Corruption has been a concept for academics to conceptualise the overall dimensions of corruption and its implications in the society from micro level to macro level. Rules and regulations have proliferated to tackle the menace through institutional arrangements. Seminars, symposia, workshops and conferences are increasing in number with liberal assistance from funding agencies, both governmental and non-governmental, to ponder over this issue. Commissions and committees have been appointed continuously. Newspapers are carrying a heavy load of information about the corrupt practices of the politicians and bureaucrats. Politicians, irrespective of their stature and character, make use of the charges framed against their opponents to destabilise them. Inquiries and investigations are on. Tons of reports have been submitted to the appropriate authorities ceremoniously for prompt action. Steps are on through due process to book the corrupt individuals and yet none has been punished and people are not freed from corruption. People's agony continues to grow in the midst of the steps taken by the government. Corruption has percolated into the body politic, administrative system and society very deeply and its anchorage is strong. It has totally uprooted the values of the society. Against this background what can be done at the micro level is thought of as something that has to be initiated to contain corruption.

Why This Spurt in Corruption?

Corruption, as a major phenomenon in the political sphere, has been discussed for a long time. Even before 1990, corruption had been on the agenda of the political parties, especially during the time of election. This type of outburst among the political parties has sometimes provoked the administration to act on the papers submitted by the leaders of various political parties. As a result, in the middle of the 1980s, a 12 volume series entitled *Committees and Commissions on Corruption* was published. Yet there was no serious debate among the academics on this issue and there was no initiative of any professional body to tackle this problem. But now a new intellectual trend has been set in motion in Indian academia. Why this fever now among the intellectuals?

A Lead from Lending Agency

As long as the money generated from within was put in the pipeline for various activities of the government and there were leakages in the pipeline (leakage or seepage has to be decided on the quantum of money that has been siphoned off from the pipeline), none paid serious attention to it. This intellectual trend has been the outcome of a serious deliberation on the part of a funding agency which has pumped a huge amount of money for development activities into our country. When the flow of money was not properly channellised and was mismanaged, the funding agencies expressed their anguish and dissatisfaction. Against this background, this phenomenon has been incorporated in the reports of their organizations.

Funding agencies, with their grants to various institutions, sensitized the scholars who have been under the influence of the classical liberal school, especially from the West. Why this fever only from this school? It is an open argument that funds have been allocated liberally by the funding agencies from the West, especially the USA, to the academic institutions. There is yet another question: does it mean that the other school in social sciences, namely the Marxist, is silent on it and has not taken any effort? It is not so.

Why have the academics of this school with funding from the Indian State not taken serious consideration of the problems? The answers are twofold: (1) the State has not provided so much of money for this kind of exercise due to its reluctance as it would destabilize the government itself; (2) the majority of Indian academics have switched over to the victorious school of classical liberalism after the end of an ideology, namely after the collapse of communism in Russia. Though piecemeal studies were conducted individually and published in journals, these did not evoke the expected reaction from the academia. It could be noticed even in the trend report of the ICSSR, which has not projected this problem as a major issue or item for investigation.

Masking Conceptualization

Normally the academics who belong to the classical liberal school of the West go about any issue based on clearcut conceptualization. In the case of corruption, after the publication of the World Bank report, corruption became a significant issue for discussion. To them, leakage of money in the implementation process of programmes is corruption. When enormous amounts of money are being spent on various programmes of development, the funding agencies expect results as an end product of their investment. In this connection, they have pointed out corruption in terms of money taken out of the process. Since funding has been provided by the same agencies to discuss the dimensions of corruption with a set of objectives, our academics have taken up this issue without proper grounding in the form of suitable theory as they lack proper conceptualization.

Normally any violation of established law to perform a function in a given role of an individual is to be considered for the definition of the concept of corruption. Likewise any violation of social norm accepted by the community can also be considered corruption. Laws, rules and regulations have been changed based on the pressure of the community. Social norms continue to face challenges in the society in the context of social change and modernization.

When social values and common laws are getting changed, the possibility for anchorage of any such definition is remote. At present there are established propositions like that corruption increases the speed of the organizations and institutions in terms of their output. Yet another question is how laws and values are regarded by the people. This aspect has to be studied deeply.

How do we assess whether the citizens are abiding by the rules and regulations of the society and government or not? It is ultimately dependent on the nature of the state and perception of the people about a problem. When Gandhiji expressed his opinion about corruption at the dawn of Independence, nobody worried about it. When commissions were constituted to probe the allegations against the government, people believed that, based on the findings of the commissions and committees, action would be initiated against the guilty. But things went different after the submission of the reports by the commissions. The reports became issues for politics. The authority which constituted the committees and commissions had the power to take or not to take action on the findings of the committees. Every time we hear the political rhetoric that action will be initiated to book the guilty. So far none has been booked as the State is soft.

Pratap Singh Kairon was one of the best Chief Ministers during the period of Nehru, as he laid the foundation for a prosperous Punjab. But allegations were brought against him. Likewise, Tamil Nadu has been adjudged as the first state in implementing social welfare programmes and considered the best pro-poor State according to the Tenth Finance Commission. A Certificate of Excellence was awarded to the concerned Minister and she was booked within a couple of months, as she was involved in large scale corruption in the same portfolio of social welfare. How do we conceptualise these paradoxes? The offices of the President and the Prime Minister are no exceptions. Leakage of information to foreign agencies has been traced and some officials have been dropped from key positions and yet the same officials have got higher positions later. How does this happen in the system when it functions within the framework of rules and regulations?

Wards of ministers, secretaries and executives of business houses are pursuing their educational programmes in western countries by investing huge sums of money in the belief that western institutions are known for quality. How was it possible for them to send their wards to western countries for their studies with huge amount of investment? After retirement, the secretaries of many departments take up assignments in foreign countries and serve for many years to the satisfaction of the concerns. How is it possible for them to get such high positions in the business houses of western countries?

I have quoted these issues just to indicate the paradoxes in the Indian political and administrative system. This needs a total review and proper conceptualization. This has been time and again urged by two eminent intellectuals, namely M.N. Srinivas and Rajni Kothari in their speeches and writings. They have also maintained that evolving a framework to study corruption should be based on the moral ethos of our country and not on the framework given by the funding agencies of the West. Thus, the need of the hour, is proper conceptualization.

The Problem

Corruption as a concept is perceived and explained by individuals differently and, accordingly, different notions have been developed. It has been interpreted in two different dimensions, namely legal and moral. Politicians talk much about legal corruption and scholars discuss both. The problem we undertake is inclusive of both. The whole perspective of the analysis emanates from a very basic question: to what extent do the activities of the government affect the livelihood of the people at present and in the future? It is not getting bribe alone or doing favours to a few individuals. It goes beyond that. Actions of the individuals, collectivities, organizations, institutions and governments are to be seen from a broader perspective of the implications and consequences of the actions to the people and the resources at their disposal.

Corruption at the micro level at present has created a hope to the politicians of the provincial polity that they need not worry about the non-devolution of powers since they get huge amounts of money while administering development. Likewise, the development functionaries also thrive on corruption. It is obvious from the life style and standard of life of the politicians and the officials that they are leading a luxurious life beyond their means and hence unethically earned money is being spent. The nexus between politicians and the development functionaries is strong. In the development process, the actions of the politicians and the development functionaries have affected the people in the rural areas. The middle class and the upper middle class have found ways and means to escape from these corrupt practices of the politicians and the officials. Sometimes they too are involved in the process. But, ultimately, the poor are the victims and they are ignorant and unorganized. They are being exploited by many. It is a paradox that, while India has more number of programmes for the poor, underprivileged, marginalized and weaker sections than other countries, yet the poor become poorer and poorer while the rich become richer and richer. How can this happen? To find out the answer to this question a study has been conducted in a small village and the Village Panchayat has been taken as an experimental one to make it a model. The present write-up is a narration of this experiment.

Conceptual Analysis

The whole issue of corruption has to be seen against the backdrop of the state and the society. Corruption is not a new issue to Indian society and for that matter, the whole world. It has its own legacy in the historic past. Many premiers have been prosecuted and independent commissions have been constituted in many countries of the world. In general terms corruption is seen as a deviation of behaviour from the normal code of conduct laid down by the society. Now it is defined as utilising public office for private gain. Corruption is not an exclusive phenomenon of any country. It is a disease afflicting all the societies in the world. The range and the quality may vary from society to society. Corruption has been visualised as the misuse of state power. In every respect corruption starts from the government because of the individuals who manage the government. Payoffs are huge at higher levels. It becomes a practice that percolates into the entire system of governance. Policy environments and execution environments provide opportunities for corruption. The causative factors are many.

It is true that the higher the financial flow, the higher the proportion of corruption. When economic programmes are activated to achieve higher growth and consequent development, simultaneous efforts should also be made to check the misuse of power and the flow of money. The developed countries have also experienced the same trend as India does today. But they have overcome this through various corrective measures through institutional and behavioural arrangements. India has been ranked number seven in terms of its level of corruption. Tamil Nadu is concerned that the whole polity of the province is polluted by corruption. In the midst of this problem, Gandhigram Rural Institute has initiated an action plan as repeatedly urged by Sri.C.Subramaniam, the elder statesman of India, to make a small attempt to eradicate corruption at micro level or at least to contain corruption.

A Micro Experiment

To move from the domain of knowledge to that of action, an area was chosen and an individual was selected. Vadugambadi, a Village Panchayat, and its president Mr. Perumal was selected for this task. Vadugambadi is a service village of the Department of Political Science and Development Administration of GRI and hence, it was felt that this exercise could be done here. It is the considered opinion of all that corruption can be contained and eliminated only by a joint venture of the people and the government. Moreover, corruption is not a 'one way' process but a two way process. Corruption is not only demanding but also inducing to demand as well as patronising the practice. To curb this 'two way' practice it was felt that it is necessary to evolve an institutional mechanism and to involve the people as a community.

Mr. Perumal, a young and committed Gram Panchayat President with a communist background, came forward to perform this exercise in his Panchayat, as he commands the respect and regard of the people because of his transparent activities in the Panchayat. It is a Panchayat reserved for SC and he got elected in a contest with the support of all the communities. It is worth noting that he is recognized by all caste leaders in his Panchayat and hence this Panchayat has been selected for this venture.

All the caste leaders from Vadugambadi Panchayat, alongwith the elected members of the wards of the Panchayat, including the President and the Vice-President, were invited to a preparatory meet in Gandhigram Rural Institute. About eighty members participated in the preparatory meeting. Since the objectives of the meet were clear, the meeting did not take much time for briefing. After the introductory remarks of the Vice-Chancellor of the Institute, groups were formed to identify the sufferings of the people in the rural areas due to corrupt practices prevalent in the governance and to suggest remedies and solutions to protect the people from this evil practice. The first group indicated the areas in which corrupt practices were prevalent, affecting the rural folk:

1. The Revenue Department, especially its officials, namely *Tahsildar,* Revenue Inspector and Village Administrative Officer are corrupt bullies demanding money for each and every certificate people seek from them, whether it is income certificate or community certificate or heir certificate. When they seek any certificate without giving money, they cannot get the same. For every certificate there is a fixed price. As everyone knows this practice, however, poor he may be, he has to prepare himself to pay the amount to get things done. Yet another area for money making for the Revenue Department personnel is issuing of ration card. Even in genuine cases, they demand money. From the entire village no one has obtained the card without giving money to the concerned officials. Extra cards have been given to many individuals after getting money from them. Thus, it is a money spinning exercise for the revenue officials.
2. Police stations trigger conflict among individuals and groups and then, to settle the same, they demand money from both the groups and individuals. Police stations have brokers for

mediation. Poor people in the villages do not know how to approach the police station to settle disputes. As long as it is confined to the village itself it is not a problem. If somebody goes to the police station, that is the beginning of an exercise to invite the police into the village. The police use the ignorance of the people to their advantage and finally nobody gains out of the interference of the police in the settlement of disputes. The peaceful atmosphere of the village is disturbed because of the police intervention.

3. The Block Development Office and its officials are corrupt to the core. They demand money individually and collectively from the individual beneficiary and the entire village for the benefits they bring through schemes and programmes. Here also organized brokers are functioning. They have fixed rates for each and every scheme. If it is the Single Light Scheme how much money to be given to the broker and how it is distributed and to whom it is distributed are pre-determined. Likewise, *Indira Awaas Yojana,* IRDP and other programmes are offered by the government and people do not know how to apply and what the eligibility conditions are to get the benefits. Their ignorance is conveniently exploited by the brokers. Moreover, the schemes and their details are not available in print for circulation. People do not know how to apply and to whom to apply. From the attender to the Development Officer, commission money is shared. Even after the installation of the elected Panchayats in position of power, the officials demand bribe without any fear. Thus, corruption has become an accepted phenomenon in administering development.

4. The ration shop is yet another area where large scale corruption takes place by which the entitlement of the poor is denied. The essential commodities are not distributed to all the needy families. Influential individuals in the villages get the rations of many. Sometimes the commodities are sold in the private market. Further, even if the articles are distributed to card holders, the measures are not correct. The quota of the poor is enjoyed by the rich in the villages.

5. Natural resources of the rural areas have been exploited by the rich for their own advantage, for which government has been helpful and officials have been supportive. Natural resources are the entitlements of the people who live in the area irrespective of their status.

The second group went deep into the domains of both the aspects, namely beneficiaries and adversaries. Corruption exists not only due to the taker but due to the giver also. To reduce or to end corruption, both should take place simultaneously, namely giver should stop giving bribe and taker should stop taking bribe. Where to begin is the question. They themselves admitted that, on most of the occasions, the givers, for their own advantage, persuaded the takers to accept bribes as they are getting undue benefits. Having been trained in getting bribe, the takers continue to demand bribe from all. The initiative should come from the givers that they wont give bribe for getting things done illegally. When there is no giver of unlawful money there won't be any pressure from the taker. Further there should be an organized attempt at resistance to corrupt practices. It should be a mass-based one. When there is a case of corruption in any governmental organization – it has to be opposed collectively with the support of the masses.

Based on their deliberations, they resolved to publicise through various means that Vadugambadi Panchayat is a corruption-free village and that its people will not give bribe for getting things done. Then they resolved to constitute a people's committee with the support of the Panchayat to ensure intervention, wherever, the problem of corruption crept into Vadugambadi village. Whenever, cases of corruption was reported, an organized attempt was to be made to resist it. As a first step they decided to erect a very big board at the entrance of the village with the write-up *Vadugambadi–Corruption Free Village People's Panchayat.* Further it was to be published in the popular newspapers that the whole village has resolved to fight corruption. Thus, steps have been taken to contain corruption at the micro level. It can be a model to other Panchayats.

Follow up Action

One has to recognize the effort taken by an institution to change the mind-set of the people. The leaders are also very positive and cooperative and hence, they help the Gram Panchayat President. Further one has to appreciate the role played by the media which have given excellent coverage in their newspapers and thereby alerted the officials. Now certificates are issued without any bribe by the village administrative officer. It is a major victory for the people. This has been achieved after the repeated warnings given by the president through the Panchayat. For all development schemes of the government a fixed sum had to be given to the officials, otherwise the schemes would not be sanctioned. This problem has also been overcome by repeated highlighting of this issue by the media. The Panchayat is submitting proposals and clearing the proposals with the offices concerned as per norms. The public distribution system has been streamlined through this collective effort. Thus, it is proved beyond doubt that, through community effort, corruption could be driven out from the lower level of administration.

Conclusion

Corruption has to be dealt with at different levels. Corruption at any level will have its own effect on the society. Corruption at the micro level certainly will affect the poor and the marginalised. Any Ombudsmanic institutionalised structure can contain corruption at the macro level. At the micro level the collective effort of the community will contain corruption very effectively. It requires support from outside agencies and the leader of the community should have the will power to withstand pressure. Constant socialization of the people is an imperative need. To wipe out corruption, simultaneous efforts should be made from above and below. It calls for a mass movement. The Vadugambadi experiment is an eye opener for all Panchayats to contain corruption at the micro level.

REFERENCES

1. G. Palanithurai, Grassroot Level Corruption: A Cursory Analysis, in G. Palanithurai (ed.), *New Panchayati Raj System: Status and Prospects,* (New Delhi: Kanishka Publishers & Distributors, 1996).
2. G. Palanithurai, *Containing Corruption: A Micro Experiment,* (Gandhigram: Rajiv Gandhi Chair for Panchayati Raj Studies, 1998).
3. World Bank, *World Development Report 1997: The State in a Changing World,* (Delhi: Oxford University Press, 1997).
4. B. K. Nehru, The Roots of Corruption, *The Hindu* (23 December 1981).
5. Prem Shankar Jha, Corruption and Nation-Building I&II, *The Hindu* (4,5. September 1997).
6. Achin Vanaik, India's 50 Year Record, *The Hindu* (26 August 1997).
7. C. Subramanian, An Agenda for Action I&II, *The Hindu* (18,19 July 1997).
8. Special Correspondent, CM Stresses Corruption-free Administration, *The Hindu* (12 June 1996).
9. N. Kalyana Sundaram, Corruption, the Key Issue, *The Hindu* (29 April 1996).
10. V. R. Krishna Iyer, The Indian Elections I&II, *The Hindu* (24,25 March 1996).
11. Era. Sezhiyan, Accountability of Political Parties, *The Hindu* (22 March 1996).
12. V.R. Krishna Iyer, Lawful Corruption, *The Hindu* (17 October 1995).
13. Prem Shankar Jha, Corruption and Economic Reform, *The Hindu* (20 August 1994).
14. C.V. Narasimhan, Needed an Ombudsman, *The Hindu* (16 August 1994).
15. C.V. Narasimhan, Spread of Corruption, *The Hindu* (15 August 1994).
16. P.K. Duraisamy, Tackling Corruption—Some Relevant, Difficult Issues, *The Hindu* (5 August 1997).
17. P.L. Prasada Rao, Needed a Mass Movement, *The Hindu* (5 August 1997).
18. Alan Dorig, Good Government and Sustainable Anti-Corruption Strategies: A Role for Independent Anti-Corruption Agencies?, *Public Administration and Development* 15 (1995).

18

CORRUPTION AND PUBLIC MORALE

B.R. DWARAKI

Preamble

Strictly speaking any writing on corruption needs no preamble. Corruption as a practice is so ubiquitous in our country and corruption as a topic has become so widely written about, that whatever one writes on corruption seems to become saleable. Yet the intention of this preamble is to stress precisely how corruption in India has influenced public morale and *vice versa.*

Corruption Institutionalized

It is paradoxical that the slogan "honesty is the best policy" co-exists with the practitioners of dishonesty making the upright ones look too ideological to be appreciated. The pragmatic world surrounding the honest people could even impute to them a lack of wisdom and prudence. So much so appreciation of honesty and a non-corrupt way of life seems to be limited to stage-managed shows, debates, discussions and seminars. Ironically enough, some of those not so wellknown for upright life (if not, outrightly corrupt) may find their way to these shows and may even organize some of them. Does this all mean that, in addition to corruption being institutionalized, people by and large have come to accept the inevitability of its existence?

Materialism *versus* Religiosity

The fact that the standard of living rather than the quality of life has set the tone for the very idea of progress has been squarely responsible for the mad scramble to make the best out of the given situation for merely oneself and one's own kith and kin. What is worse is that this craze for acquisition has made close ones become distant and even enemies. Religiosity, seen from this perspective, had all through contributed to the maintenance of acceptable levels of morality both at the individual and at the social levels. This force can be seen to be very strong in the Indian villages. A poor man, justice being on his side, may loose his piece of land and pacify himself with the conviction that, although the rich man could manage to win in the earthly courts of law, he will definitely have no chance in the court of the Almighty on the 'Day of Reckoning', because one has to speak oneself there as one can not get a lawyer to speak at any price. Such are the ways of materialism that, if one finds a big bundle of currency notes in the hundial of Lord Venkateswara, one can make an easy guess that it is certainly not from a person who made money through fair means. What a paradoxical compromise between religiosity and materialism!

Weakness for Short-cuts

Plainly speaking, a person who has time and patience at one's disposal is very unlikely to look for a short-cut. It is the attitude behind this weakness that is likely to lead to an involvement in corruption. After all, for every individual who wishes to get something done faster and easier at a price, there is at least one individual there out in the system who is ready to quote a price for doing this. In the final analysis, it is the market that settles the price of the bargain. Thus, to ask who is responsible for corruption—the giver or the taker—is as much a moot question as the proverbial hen-and-egg proposition.

Crime *vs* Sin

A very crisp definition of conscience goes thus: Conscience 'knows' what is wrong! Sigmund Freud, writing on the concept of super ego, wrote decades ago to mean what follows: if two individuals involve in something anti-social secretively and then suffer from guilt feeling, it would mean their conscience is intact; on the other hand, if they both do not suffer from any guilt feeling and are worried about a third person coming to know about it, their fear is externalised. And that is the starting point of corruption. Because, in the first case, the values are internalised, i.e., an individual becomes a sinner the moment the sin is committed. In the latter case, the very act of committing a crime can not make an individual a criminal. The entire chain of external support systems of law will have to establish so.

Inner *vs* External Peace

It will be safe to believe that, except for a negligible percentage of psychopaths and socio-paths, most normal individuals do possess the force of conscience within them. It is not without reason that Gandhiji strongly believed that every individual had the ability for self control. An upright and honest non-corrupt individual is most likely to have inner peace. But this individual is almost always at war with the corrupt world surrounding him/her. On the other hand, a corrupt person is likely to get along well with most others, but, within himself, is possibly feeling pricked. The situation in present day India demands that one make one's own choice. It is very unlikely that one can have peace on both the fronts, given the present situation in India which has obtained a world ranking in corruption.

Esoterism – the Language of Corruption

The mere fact that an individual is aware that a certain office/department/agency is corrupt does not entail on the individual the liberty of walking in and opening a deal. The prospective giver in corruption will have to have a contact person in the concerned office/department/agency. The only other alternative is to pretend innocence. But then the price tag in the latter case may be larger. By and large both giver and taker in corruption are smarter than normal people in society. In the final analysis, there develops a symbiotic relationship between the two parties that they understand each other, sometimes even without a word being spoken.

Corruption *vs* Public Morale

In the present juncture, it is not easy to argue convincingly whether public opinion is in support of or opposed to corruption. To the extent to which a substantial number get involved in corruption, it looks supportive. Yet, so long as 'honesty is the best policy' remains an ideal, one can say that public spirit is opposed to corruption. As for the takers in corruption, any right thinking individual will still not be unnerved by the very fact of the existence of corruption. What seems more dangerous is that one can quote the price referred to, the department/office/agency and perhaps even name the individual who should be offered a 'warm handshake' to get something done.

Yet the final word remains. Whereas, the corrupt ones are able to muster the support of others or even get it unasked for in the event of a crisis, the upright ones are destined to fight it alone! The pragmatic world around seems to function under an openly undeclared albeit generally acceptable policy that the honest person has been imprudent in the first place.

19

RECOMMENDATIONS OF THE WORKSHOP

Recommendations

Elimination of Corruption in Local Level Institutions

1. Working procedures for various purposes in different departments have to be reviewed and made as open as possible. The system needs to be opened up by providing a role for the society. Local people should be actively involved in planning, monitoring and reviewing periodically. This will help to demystify service delivery and empower citizens by informing them about their rights and what they should expect from the service procedures.
2. Concentration of power in a single department or authority, for example, for issuing licences, permits and a variety of certificates like fitness certificate, no objection certificate, community certificate, birth certificate, etc., promotes corruption. Such corruption can be considerably reduced if the power of issuing such certificates is dispersed among more than one authority wherever possible. Specific items for such dispersal of powers have to be identified. All certificates such as caste, occupation, residence and income have to be issued only by the Panchayat ward member, countersigned by the Village Panchayat president. A register of such certificates has to be maintained by the Panchayat. Such a practice was prevalent in the French Territory in India till 1968.
3. Decentralization must not stop with the elected leaders of the Panchayat. In the name of Panchayat, a new set of *Zamindars*

must not be created at village level. In the existing social structure, decentralization has to be carefully fitted to accommodate the interests of the most deprived.

4. Decentralization to the level of the weakest section must be effected and reservation will not serve the purpose. 'Power to people' must be effected by recognizing the need for several types of functional groups working at the operational level. The concept of co-management by empowering new groups, self-help groups, and groups of socially deprived people within the larger framework of the Panchayati Raj System has great scope. Once people are empowered and capacitated, the demand for transparency and accountability will come from below.
5. Performance audit system may be introduced in addition to the statutory audit of local bodies. This is a running audit which is more corrective and helpful than fault finding in order to achieve the objective of detecting problems as and when they crop up.
6. Social audit may also be introduced in the local bodies. For this purpose, the Gram Sabha/ward committee should be empowered to get all the relevant details of project implementation. Gram Sabha, if it deems it necessary, can examine the records, reports and other details of project implementation. Gram Panchayats can work out the modalities of social audit.
7. The present system of treating the Village Panchayats as agencies for implementing schemes formulated by the State and Central Government should be replaced by a new system of Village Government centred in the Panchayat with full autonomy.
8. All work carried out in the village by Government Departments, NGOs, Cooperatives, Banks, etc. should be done with the approval of the Village Panchayat.
9. All development schemes of the village have to be formulated only by the Panchayat.
10. The Panchayat should have power to modify the schemes of State/Central Governments and other apex bodies to the specific needs of the village and implement them.

11. The Panchayat should be allowed to make use of the services of any chartered engineer for all Government Schemes.
12. Each Panchayat may be given a 'block grant' annually to take up schemes required by the village but not possible under the existing programmes.
13. Beneficiaries of all schemes should be selected only by the Gram Sabha.
14. MLAs' and MPs' fund should be channelized through Panchayats.
15. Tender system and the practice of engaging contractors have to be abolished in respect of Village Panchayat Work. A "Village Work Society" has to be organized and all the work may be implemented by this society as per the estimates prepared by the chartered engineer and approved by the Panchayat. The President of the Panchayat should not be the Director or President of the Village Work Society. For each work executed by the society, a member of the Panchayat may be deputed as the observer.
16. All the staff of all the Government Departments including Police Department may be placed under the administrative control of the Panchayat of the village.
17. For the Nutritious Noon Meal Schemes, the Government can give funds to the Panchayats. The Panchayat should implement the scheme through DWCRA Women Groups or Mahalir Mandrams of the village.
18. At present, due to lack of administrative, technical and financial power, the Village Panchayat Presidents are not able to implement schemes quickly. The Government has to give these powers to the Panchayats within 3 or 6 months to enable the Panchayats to work efficiently.
19. The Union Engineer in the Panchayat Union should be ordered to settle bills for work executed by the Panchayat within a week of receipt of the work completion certificate from the Panchayat President. If the Union Engineer fails to do so,

disciplinary action should be initiated against him for 'dereliction of duty' under the Government Servants Conduct Rules and Prevention of Corruption Act.

20. A minimum salary and pension should be paid to the president and the members of the Village Panchayat under the state budget.
21. All expenditure incurred on work by the Panchayats and all other information shall be kept open to the public of the village.

Curbing Corruption in Development Schemes

1. The Panchayat may prepare a list of households living below poverty line every year and place it before the Gram Sabha. Such a list may be discussed threadbare and be approved through a resolution passed at the Gram Sabha meeting. The list so finalised may be circulated among the Department of Rural Development, Revenue Department and the Banks. Loan and subsidies may be issued based exclusively on the list duly signed by the president of the Panchayat. No other documents need be insisted upon. This will, to a great extent, bring down the quantum of corruption normally found in individual and family based welfare programmes.
2. Various Government Departments like Rural Development, Agriculture, Animal Husbandry, Cooperation, Education. Sanitation, Health, Public Works, Revenue, Highways, Sanitation, Water and Drainage, etc. execute different programmes in villages without coordination among them. This invariably leads to duplication of work and sometimes results in overcrowding and concentration of programmes in a few villages. In order to avoid this, the Departments concerned, before preparing their annual plans, may consult the District Panchayat and prepare a District Plan. This will help in identifying and implementing plans useful for the community.
3. Though tender system is adopted in executing work, the Panchayat where the work is executed shall issue the work

completion certificate to the effect that the work completed is of satisfactory standard and has yielded the desired results. The bills may be passed for payment only after obtaining the certificate. The Panchayat which issues the certificate shall be held responsible for any omission or commission in the work completion certificate.

4. In case it is felt that the infrastructure created out of various projects/schemes are not being utilized, such infrastructure may be transferred to projects/schemes which require such infrastructure. This will help avoid unnecessary expenditure on new schemes.

5. There is a need to raise the consciousness of women so that they generate the power necessary to bring about positive changes. They have to be mobilized as a collective force so that they challenge oppressive forces. It is only through training and by discussing their own talents and abilities that women can develop self-confidence, in view of their socio-economic conditions.

Role of NGOs and Action Groups in Fighting Corruption

1. A consistent and orchestrated campaign should be pursued by social reformers for educating the people, especially the youth, against corruption at all levels. Citizen groups should be formed to tackle corruption in local areas on specific issues. Unless public action and cooperation are forthcoming, it will be very difficult to eliminate the menace of corruption.

2. People's committees with women and youth and without the Panchayat chief or members have to be set up in villages to monitor the functioning of schools, health centres, libraries and cooperatives to ensure their proper functioning.

3. Constitution of consumer groups at all levels – village to national level – may provide a watch-dog mechanism for ending corruption.

4. Rural cultural groups with the specific aim of propagating the evil effects of corruption may be formed.

5. Moral instruction must be part of the curriculum at all levels. Each district must have a 'centre' run by devoted and dedicated social workers with an objective of spreading good values among the people and creating a mass movement to fight against corruption at all levels.
6. Like-minded leaders may join together and lobby against corruption. The corrupt may be identified and ostracized.
7. Awareness programmes may be organized on the ill effects of corruption and the ways and means to curb corruption.
8. Information on all government schemes should be gathered and made available to the people. Booklets on government schemes may be published and circulated.
9. Communication and information media may be fully utilized to fight corruption.

Combating Corruption at the Macro Level

* Accountability in the present system is hierarchical, with little attention paid to the needs of the clients, namely citizens. This can be rectified by an arrangement for a critical scrutiny of the connected file by an ombudsman-like authority at the district level and at the state level. Such a facility for a close scrutiny of records by a duly constituted authority outside the department will help prevent arbitrary disposal of matters. Citizens can approach this institution not only to redress their grievance but to get compensation whenever hardship is caused by the department. The ombudsman should be a constitutionally protected statutory authority and it should follow summary procedures for disposal of complaints. It should not get bogged down in the complex web of legal formalities and procedures.
* The election system–a source of corruption – needs to be reformed. The present 73rd and 74th Constitutional Amendment Acts have led to a complicated election system. There is no organic linkage between the Gram Panchayats and the district level Panchayats. Direct election of presidents of Gram

Panchayat, Ward members of the Panchayat, chairmen of Panchayat unions, presidents of District Panchayats may help eliminate unhealthy practices in elections to local government bodies.

* Legislation to simplify the existing rules and streamline procedures in the administrative system may be necessary. It should provide new statutory powers of regulation to set and monitor standards for specific public services, fix a time frame, help make consumers aware of standards, provide for compensation when guaranteed standards are not met, improve the complaint-redressal procedure and facilitate greater competition, wherever, possible, in providing better services.

* The civil servants should be made to file annual returns of their movable and immovable properties with the government and a systematic verification of the correctness of such information should be undertaken periodically by the Vigilance Department. The disproportionate income of the civil servant and of his spouse and children should also be brought under scrutiny and prompt and appropriate action taken against illegal accumulation of wealth as per law.

* Computer communication network from village to state level may be required to move closer to the citizen. A multi – purpose citizen database with unique key number for each citizen may become necessary. The database will have the citizen's name, age, income, landholding, education, ration card number, caste and community and other relevant data required to process it for various services expected of the government department. Interlinking of departments with multipurpose connectivity up to village level has to be taken up, in a phased manner, keeping the cost factor in mind.

* Social information booths with interactive computers can be of much use to reduce corruption. The booths may provide information regarding the procedures for availing various services, eligibility conditions for getting benefits, the format of applications, government orders, the standards, the status of applications, etc. The booths can be manned by individuals and voluntary organizations.

* The Parliament, the Judiciary and the Executive must be reformed so as to become sensitive to corruption and to support its eradication.
* The institution of the Lokpal may be made mandatory at the centre as well as in the states to ensure the accountability and the transparency of the legislators. The Judiciary may be allowed to function more independently. The Chief Justice and colleagues alone should decide the appointment of High Court judges and Supreme Court judges.
* Loopholes in the judicial process should be plugged; restriction may be imposed on the number of higher appeals; judicial exemptions on flimsy grounds may be denied; any exemption should apply to all equally.
* Supreme Court need not admit flimsy appeals
* Parties' accounts must be audited. Income tax on parties funds may be imposed. Sources of funds to the parties may be made open. Ceiling on election expenses of parties should be fixed.
* No convicted person should be permitted to contest any election.
* MLAs and MPs should account for every *paisa* of the Constituency Development Grant and all expenditure under the grant shou!d be channelised through local bodies.
* No legislator/party member should be given any amnesty.
* Attendance in Parliament/Legislature has to be enforced; bebaviour on the floor has to be monitored and controlled; repeated and perverse misbehaviour should lead to disqualification from contesting in future.
* Half the seats are to be reserved for women in Parliament and legislatures to minimise the opportunity for corruption.
* Administrative powers should be decentralized below district level to the sub-district and village level.
* Principled officers should be recognized and encouraged.

Index